PETER FISCHLI
DAVID WEISS

SNOWMAN

FONDATION **BEYELER**

VERLAG DER BUCHHANDLUNG WALTHER UND FRANZ KÖNIG

In 1987, curator Kasper König invited five artists to create artworks for the Heizkraftwerk Römerbrücke, a thermal power station in Saarbrücken, Germany: Katharina Fritsch, Edward Allington, Thomas Schütte, Peter Fischli, and David Weiss. For their contribution, Fischli and Weiss proposed a work that would rely on the energy produced by the plant: a sculpture of a snowman made of actual snow generated and sustained by a cooling system inside a vitrine freezer. *Snowman* was realized in 1989 as a permanent installation.

In 2008, Fischli and Weiss redesigned *Snowman* for an unrealized project at the Walker Art Center in Minneapolis. And, in 2016, at the invitation of Susanne Ghez on behalf of the Art Institute of Chicago, *Snowman* was refabricated based on those plans. The work was then exhibited at the Art Institute of Chicago; the San Francisco Museum of Modern Art; the Museum of Modern Art, New York; the Cleveland Museum of Art; the Queensland Gallery of Modern Art, Brisbane; and Fondation Beyeler, Basel.

This book tells the story of *Snowman* in a visual essay, by Peter Fischli and Cara Manes, that charts the work's thirty-five-year history in a roughly chronological collage of images with captions and commentary. It includes plans, models, and fabrication diagrams of the sculpture, images of it in various locations, times, and states of appearance, and reference and research materials related to a broad range of topics within *Snowman*'s universe.

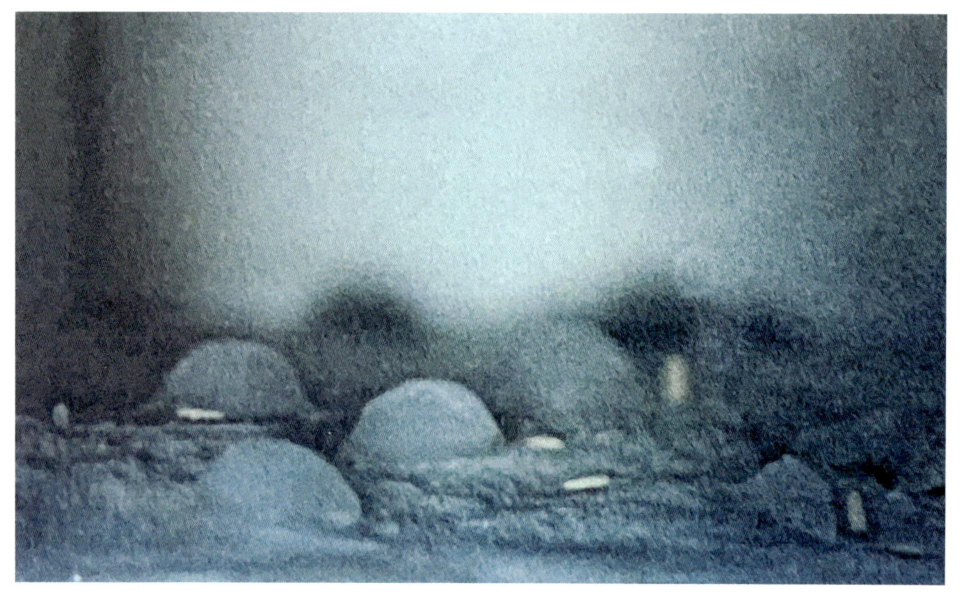

Detail, *At the North Pole*

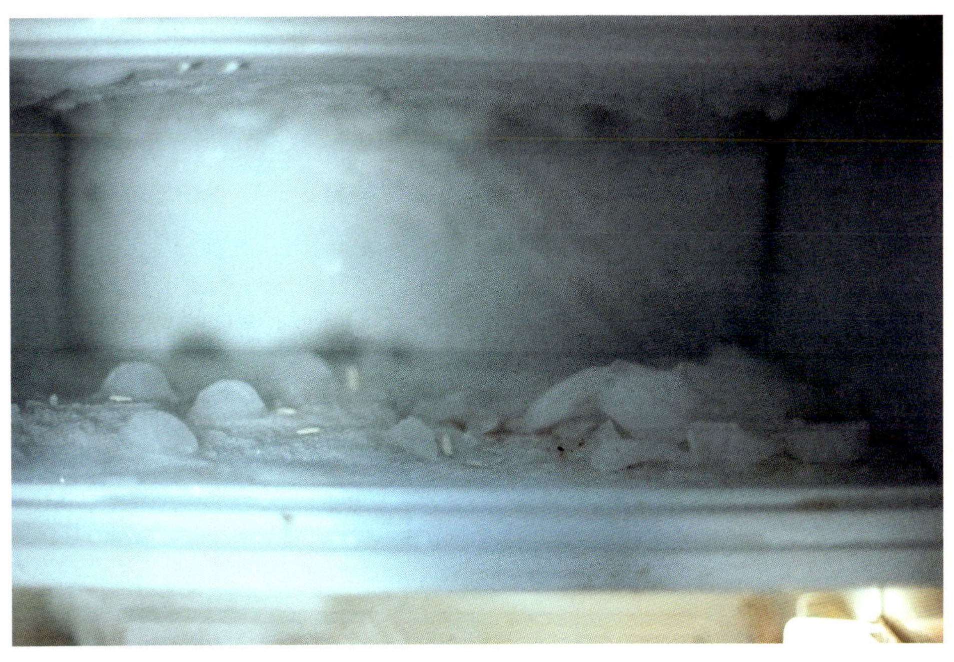

The ten photographs that comprise the *Sausage Series*, plus numerous outtakes and studies, were taken in an apartment, where household objects and a variety of sausages and other comestibles were staged in domestic locations, such as the freezer, oven, and bathtub. Peter Fischli and David Weiss, *At the North Pole*, from the *Sausage Series*, 1979. Ten photographic C-prints

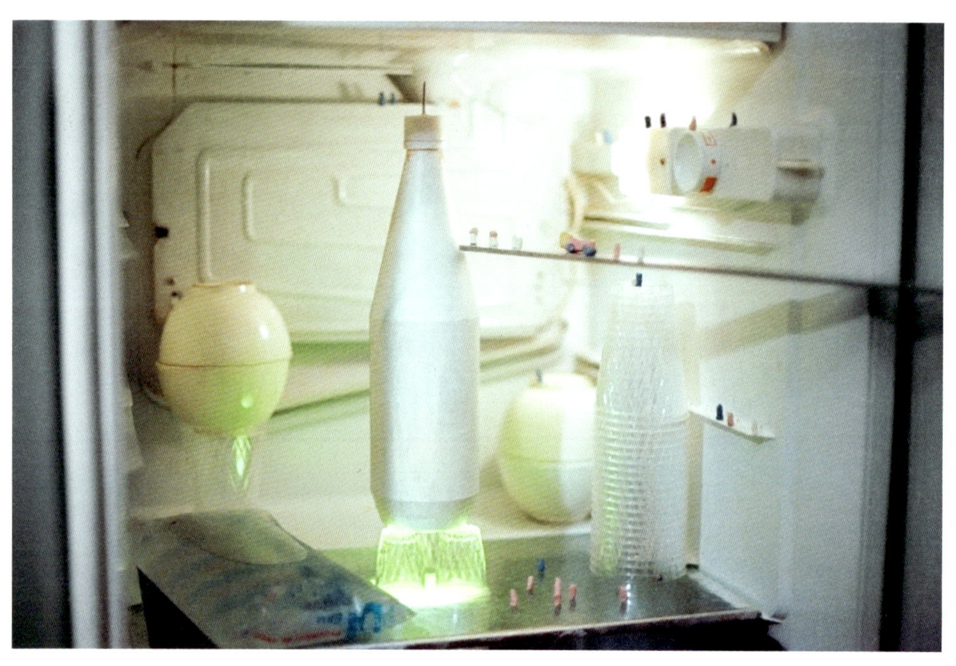

Fischli/Weiss, *Moonraker,* from the *Sausage Series*, 1979. Ten photographic C-prints

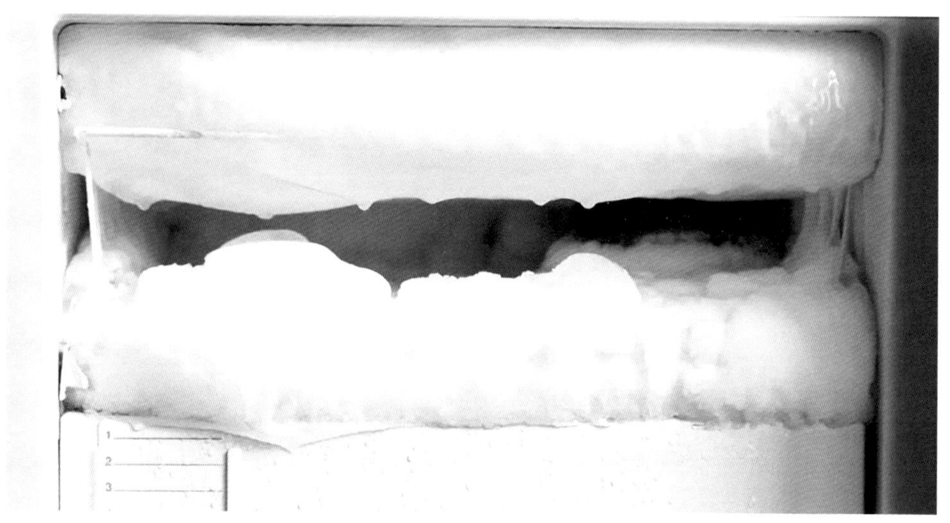

Image of out-of-control frost buildup in a domestic freezer

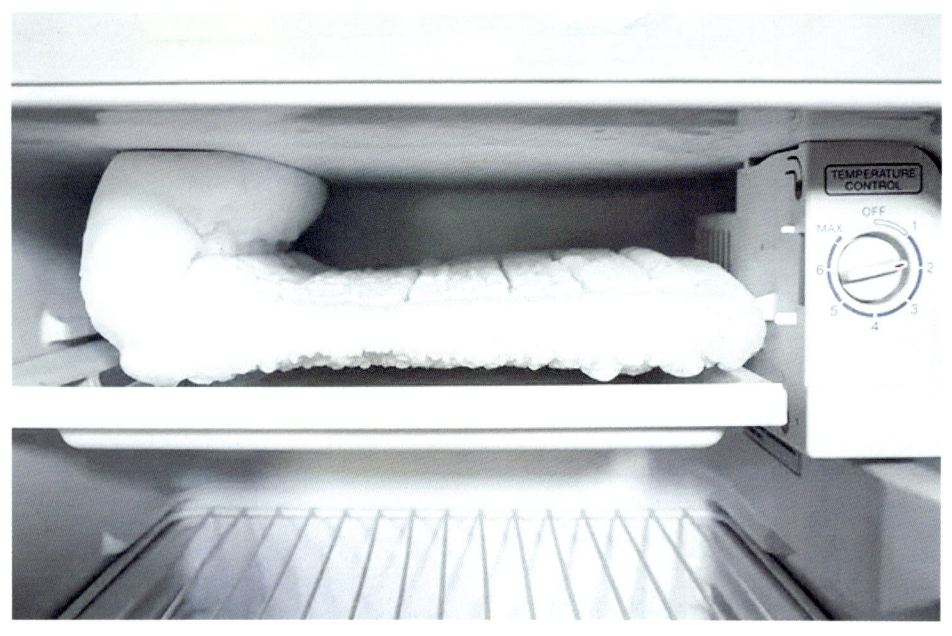

When warm or humid air makes contact with a freezer's evaporator coils, the moisture solidifies and frost forms. This is a common occurrence. Reference materials related to ice accumulation inside domestic freezers, including images found on the internet and photographs taken by the artists in their studio

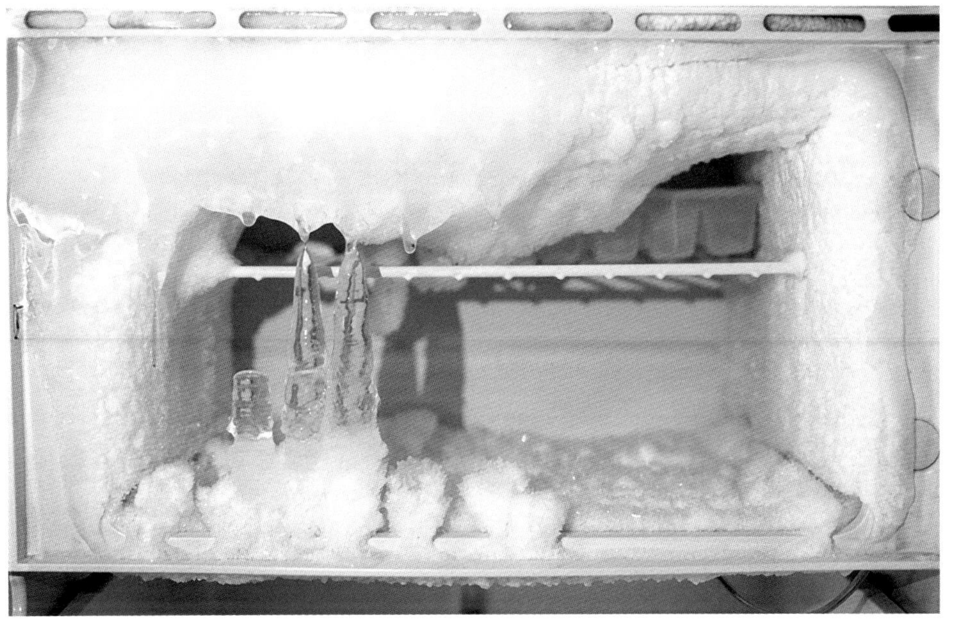

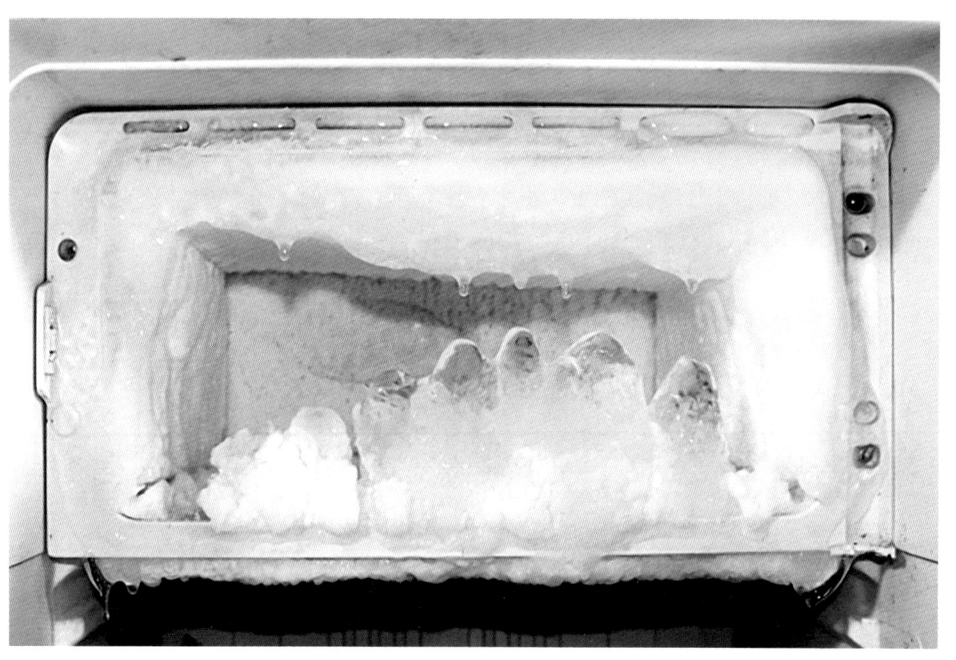

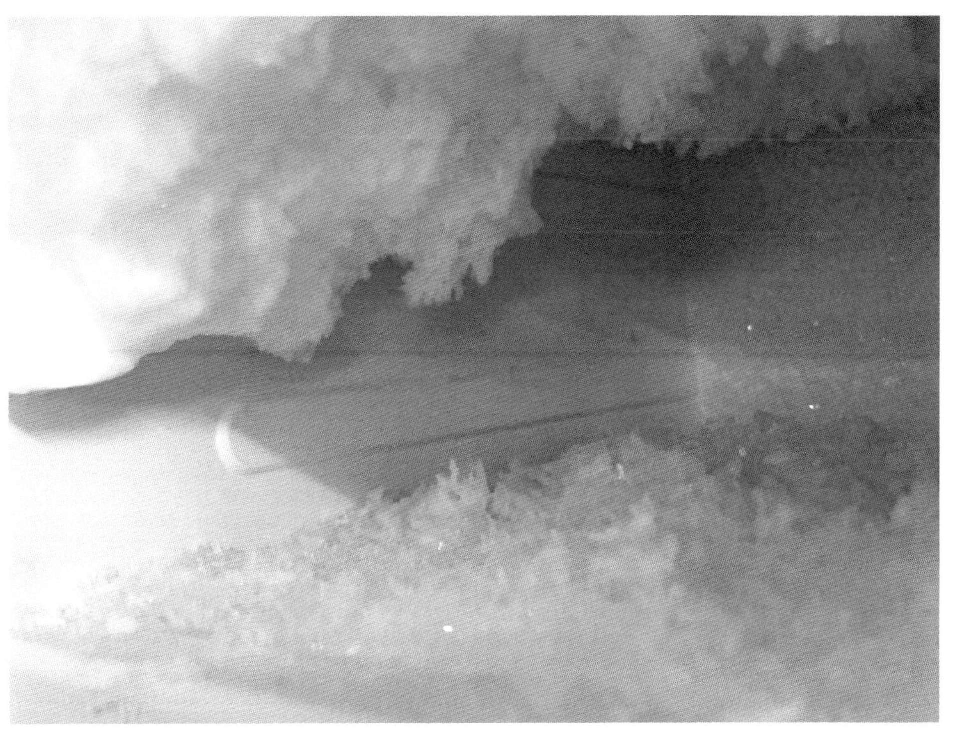

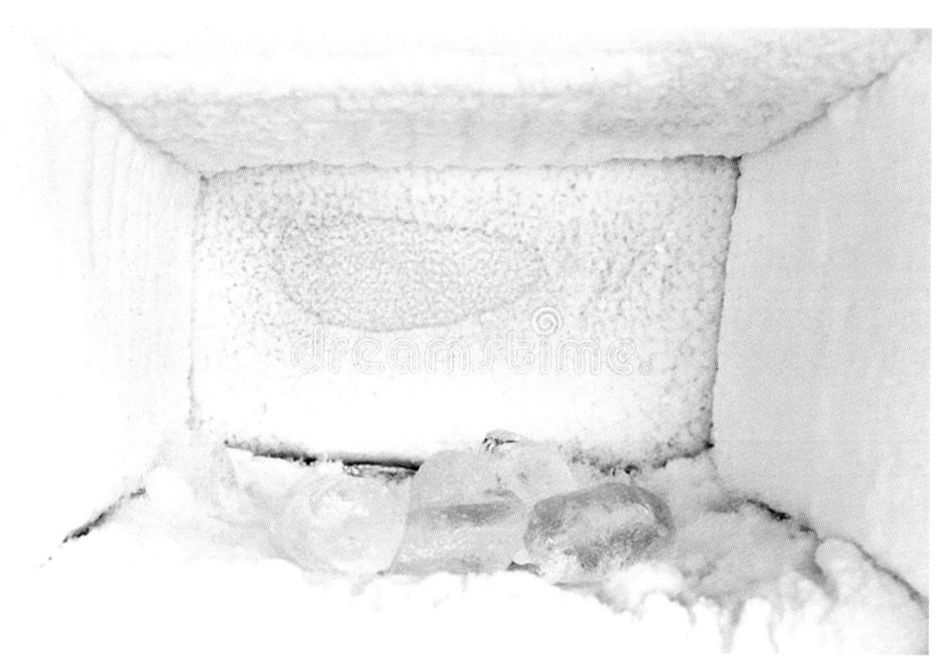
dreamstime

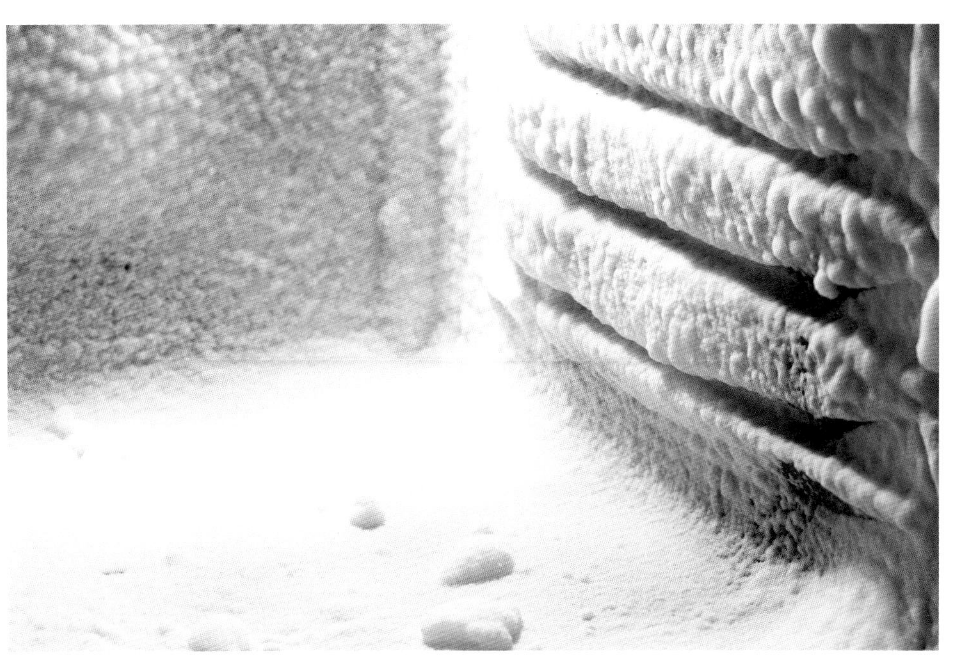

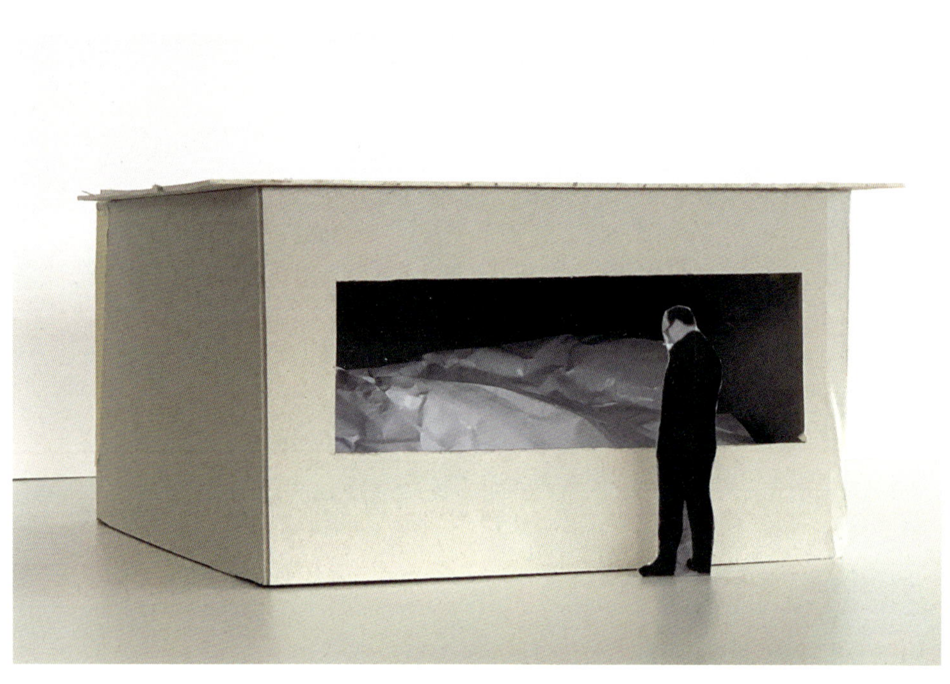

Fischli / Weiss' initial idea for the Heizkraftwerk Römerbrücke art project was a landscape made of ice housed in a cooling unit powered by the energy produced by the plant. Reconstruction of cardboard model for *Ice Landscape*, 1987. Freestanding building (500 × 350 × 250 cm) with panorama window onto an illuminated ice landscape

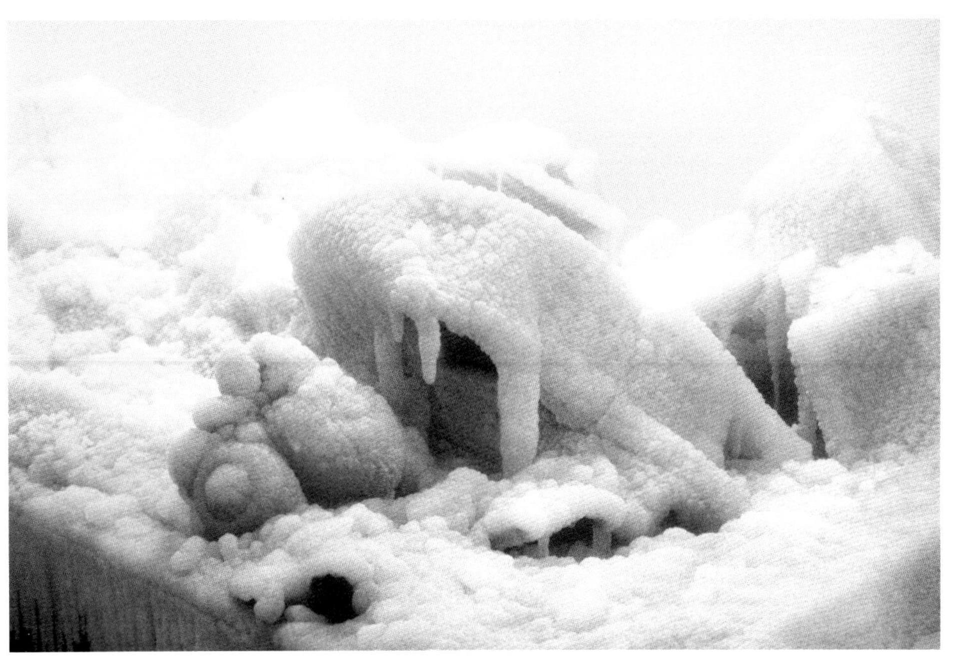

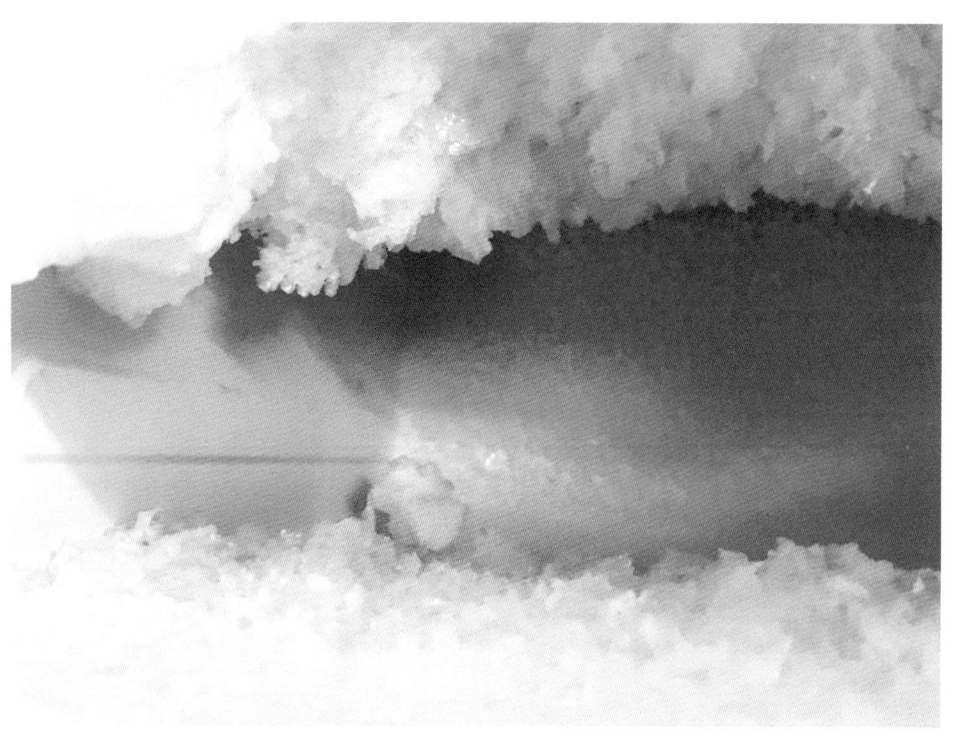

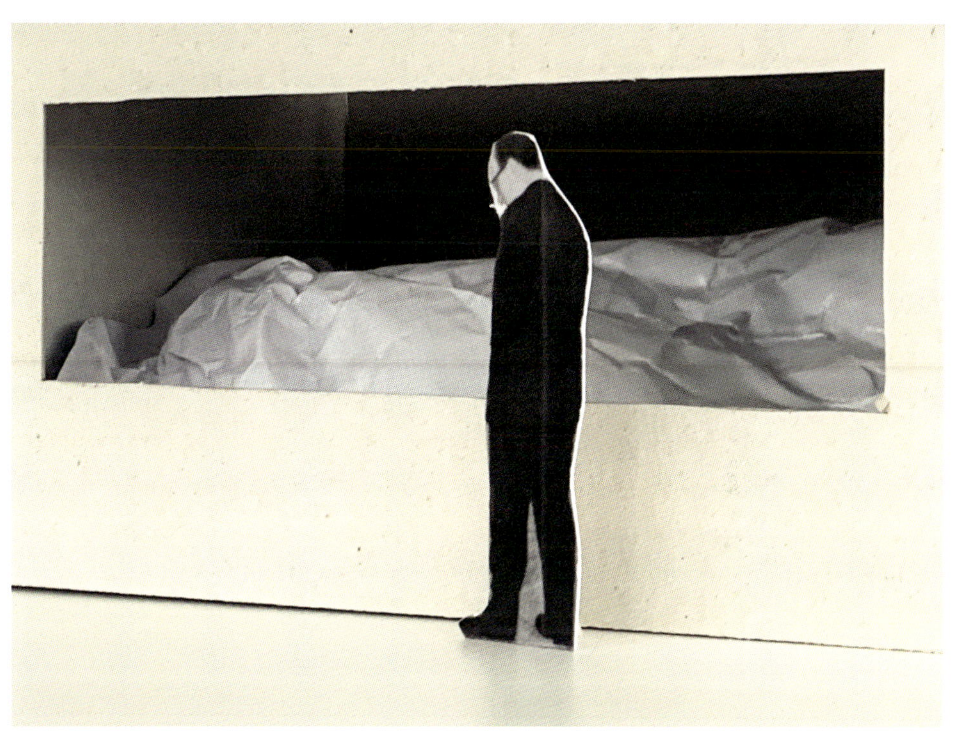

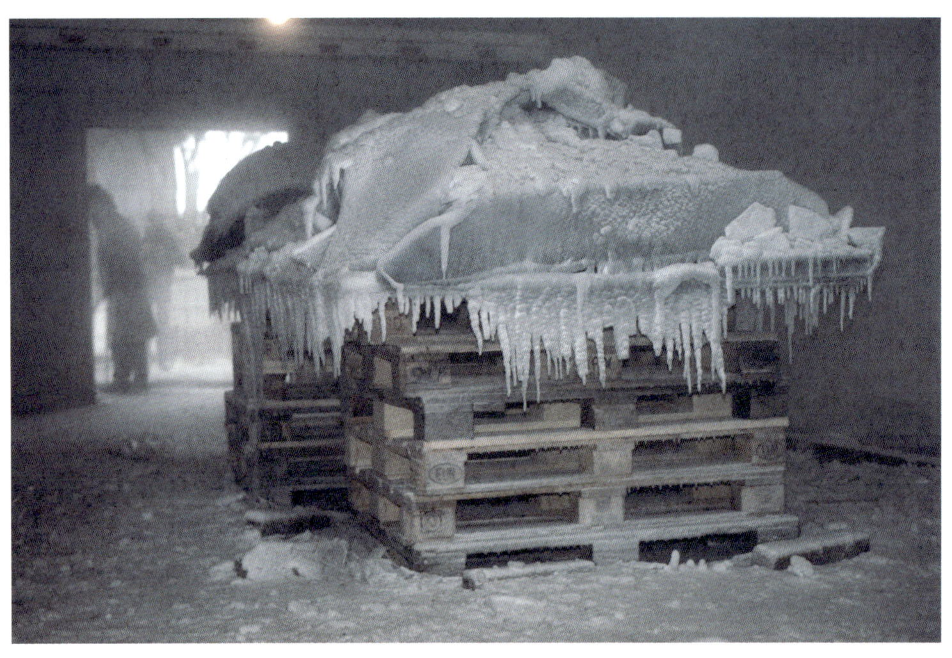

To test the viability of *Ice Landscape*, Fischli/Weiss piled scrap metal and other materials atop stacked wooden pallets inside a rented meat locker of a local supermarket chain and hosed down the resulting structure with water so that a surface of ice formed. Ultimately unrealized for the Heizkraftwerk Römerbrücke, the final project was intended to be presented as a landscape on the ground in a solitary vitrine.

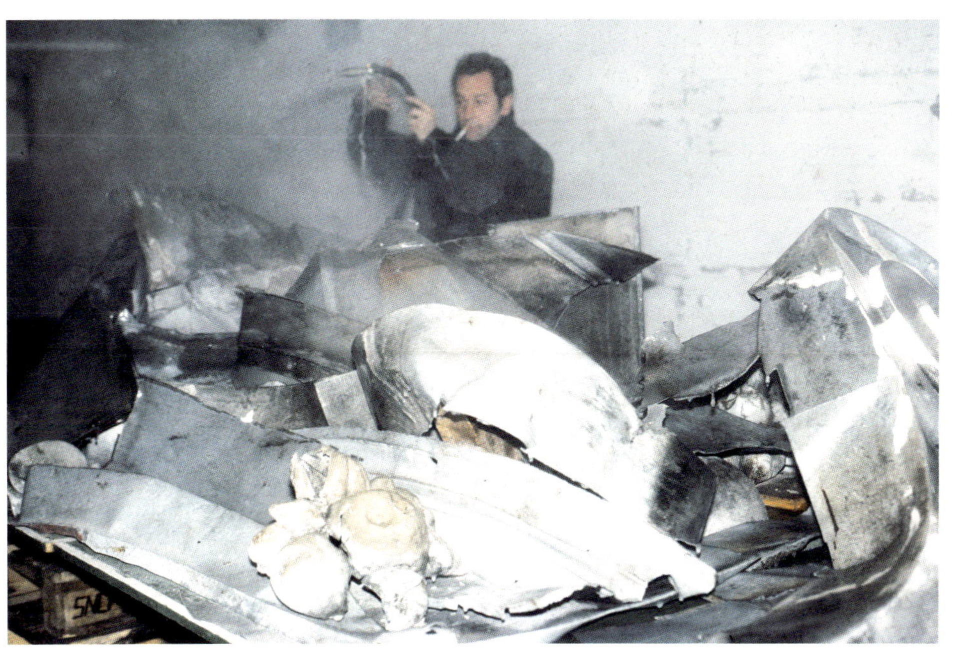

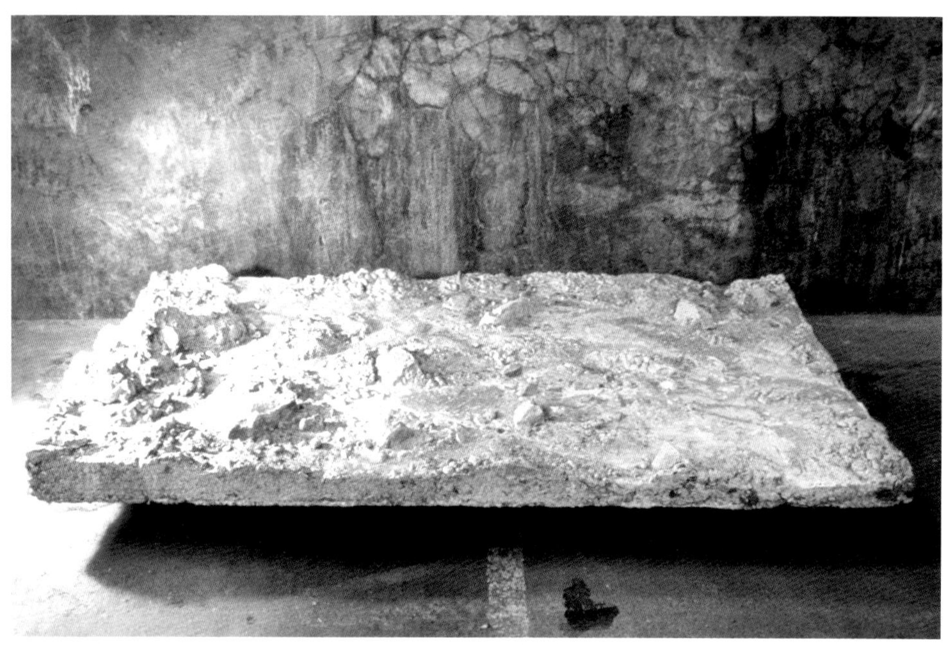

Between 1984 and 2010, Fischli/Weiss made a series of approximately fourteen sculptures by pouring viscous concrete and rock fragments in a flat rectangular mold in a manner that appeared coincidental and evoked a landscape. During the cement's thee-hour setting process, certain minor manipulations of the surface were made to achieve a sense of ambiguity between shape and shapelessness. A similar attitude guided the development of the idea for *Ice Landscape*. Fischli/Weiss, *Untitled* (from *Concrete Landscapes*), 1984

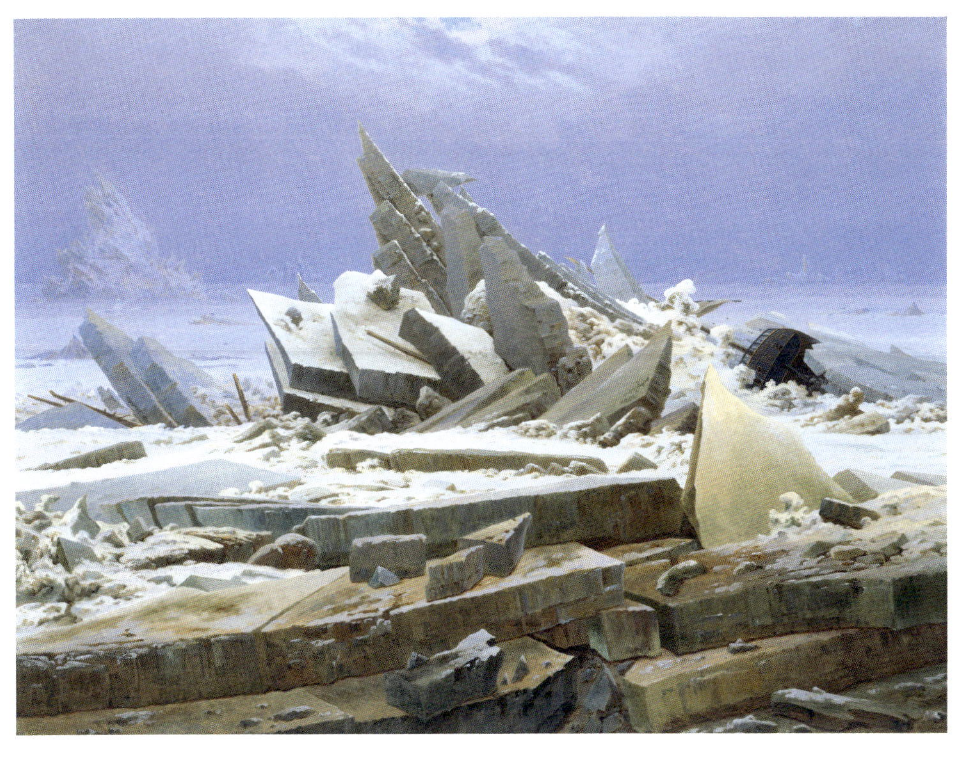

Caspar David Friedrich, *The Sea of Ice*, 1823–24. Oil on canvas. Hamburger Kunsthalle

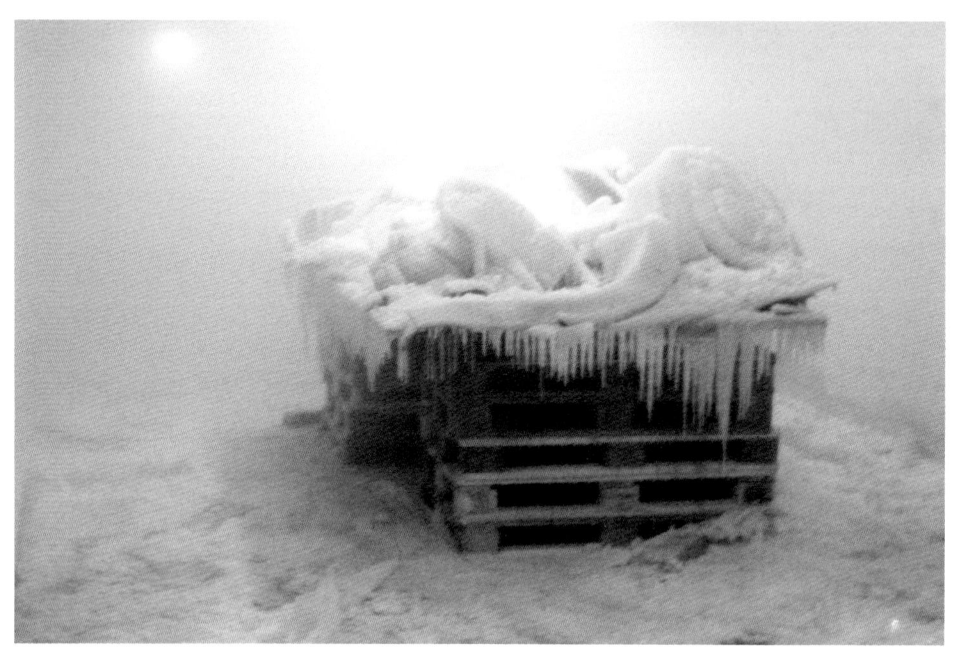

Tests for *Ice Landscape*, 1987

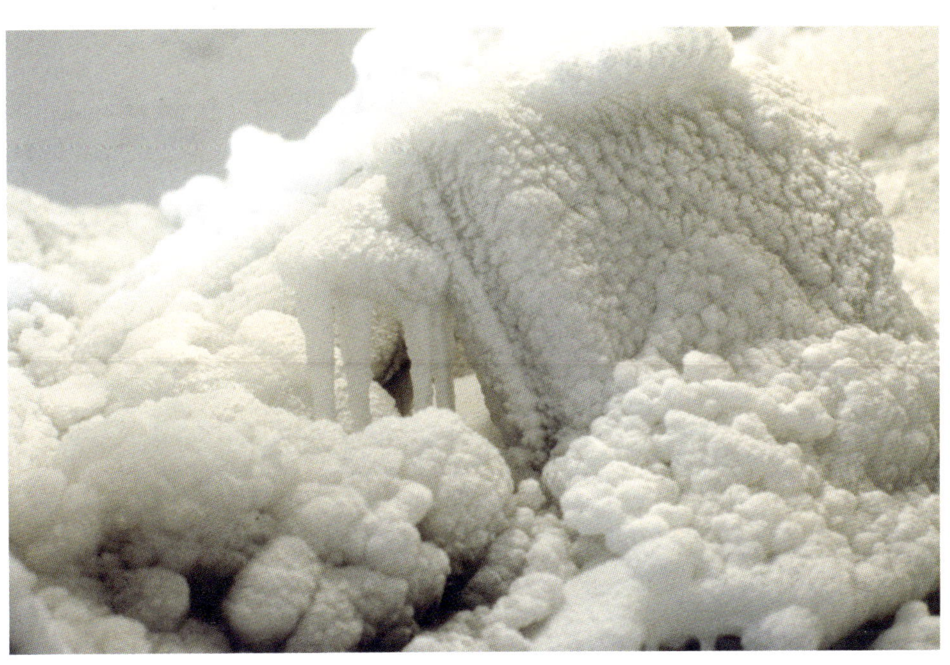

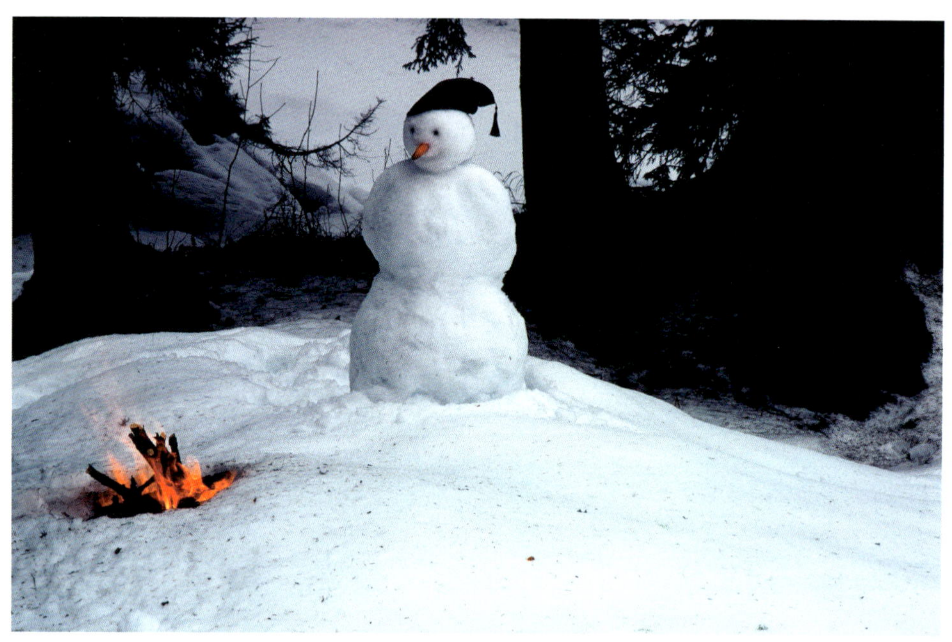

During investigations into the *Ice Landscape*, the idea for *Snowman* arose as an artwork that would also rely on the energy produced by the Heizkraftwerk Römerbrücke. Here, the powerplant serves as the snowman's lifeline, and in turn the artwork becomes completely dependent on it for survival. In place of a proper proposal, which would have included a feasibility study and construction plan, some of these images were submitted to curator Kasper König as illustrations of the idea for the commission. Upon completion of the project, one image was used as the plant's holiday card, distributed in early 1990. Selections from a series of approximately twenty-four images of snowmen in the Swiss mountains, November 1987. Photographic C-prints

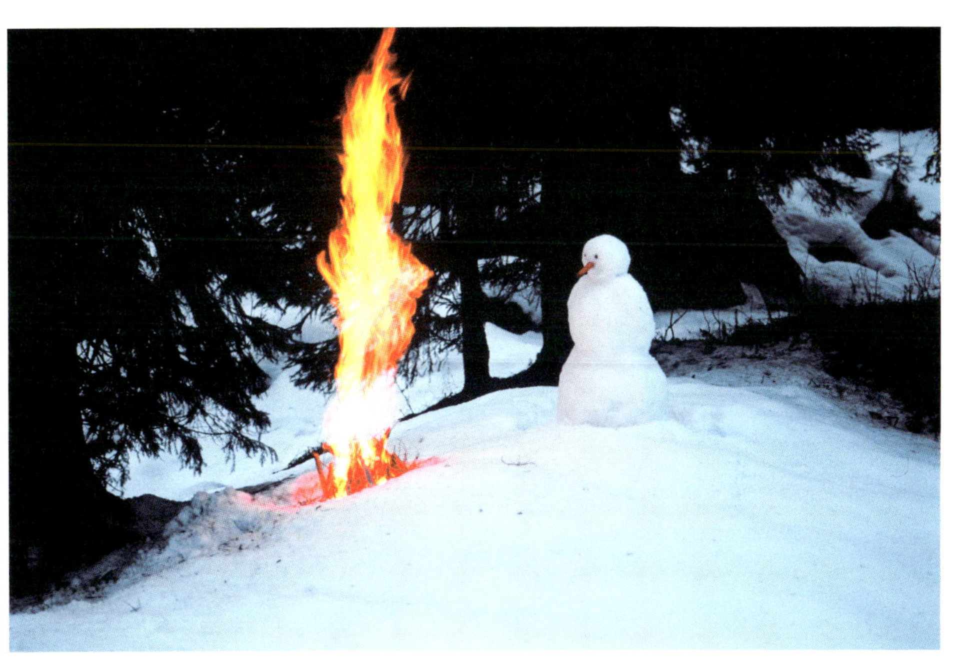

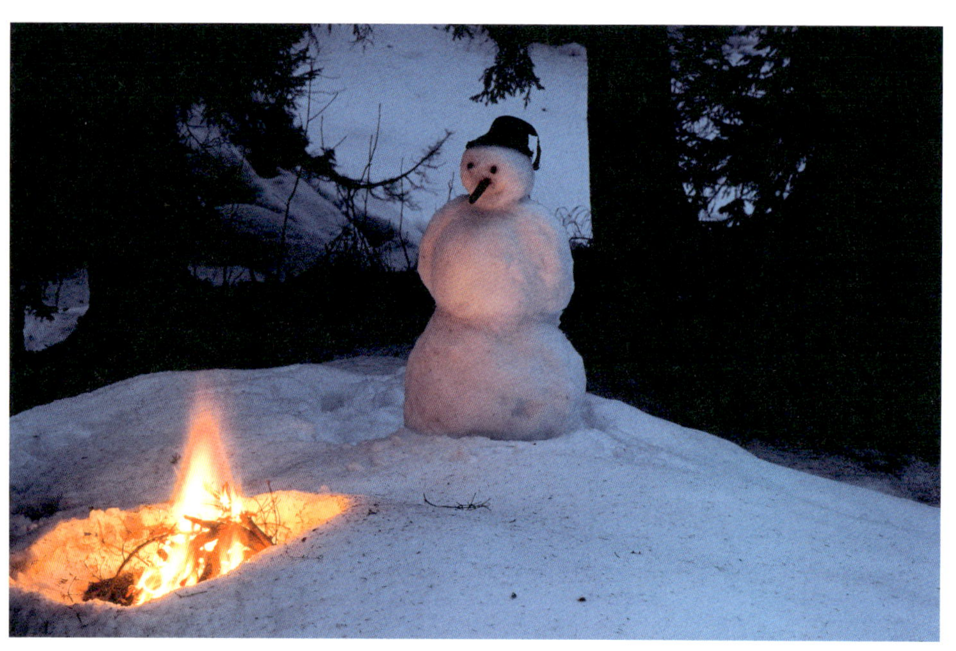

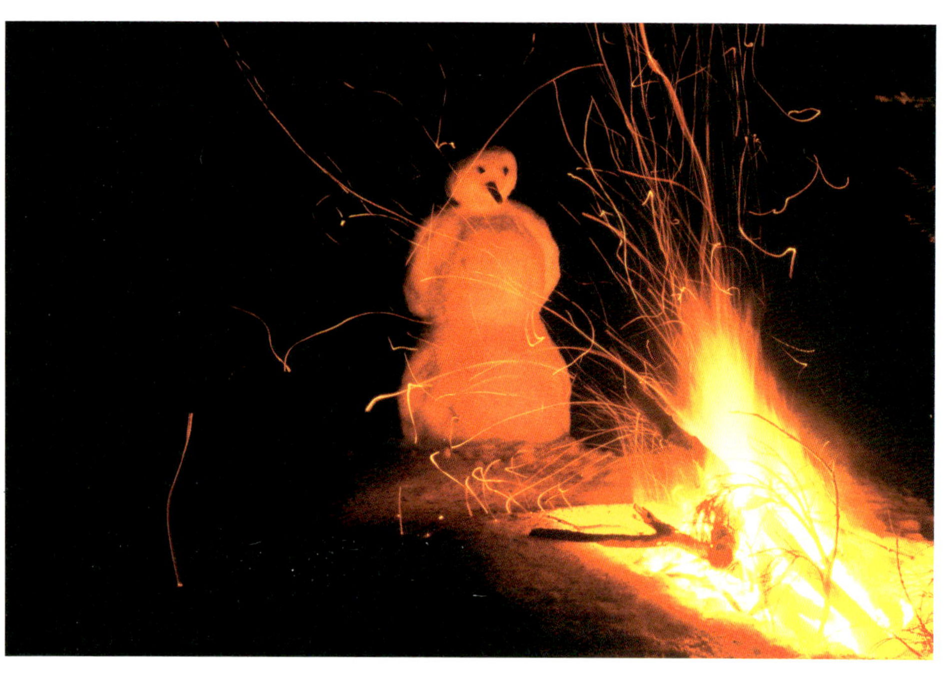

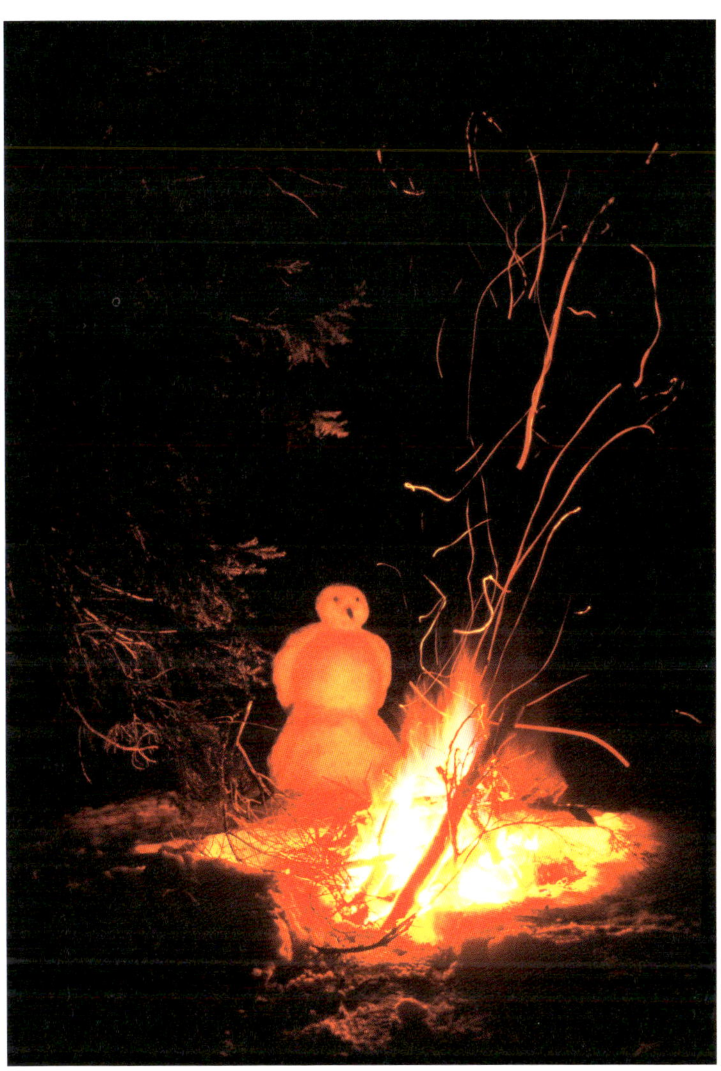

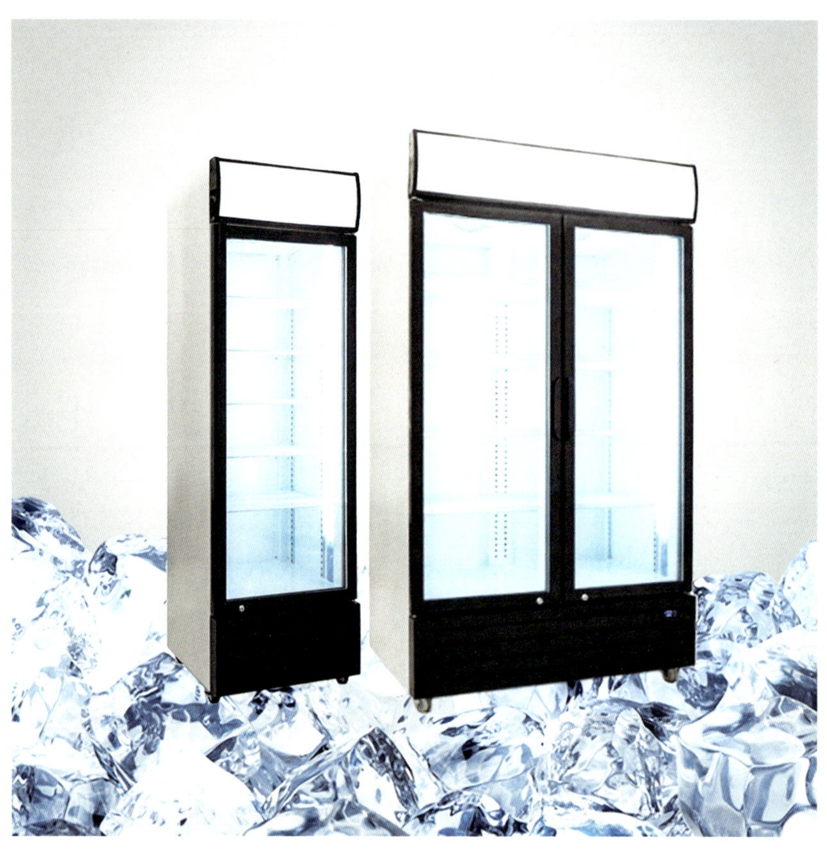

The figure of the snowman requires a container to keep it frozen through all four seasons. In the case of *Snowman*, a distinction between the sculpture and its display is impossible; they must merge in order to guarantee the snowman's *longue durée*. For this reason, research was conducted on the topic of commercial vitrine freezers typically found in restaurants for displaying cakes. Reference images of various refrigerators, freezers, and cooling units used in restaurants, shops, and households, and their energy consumption

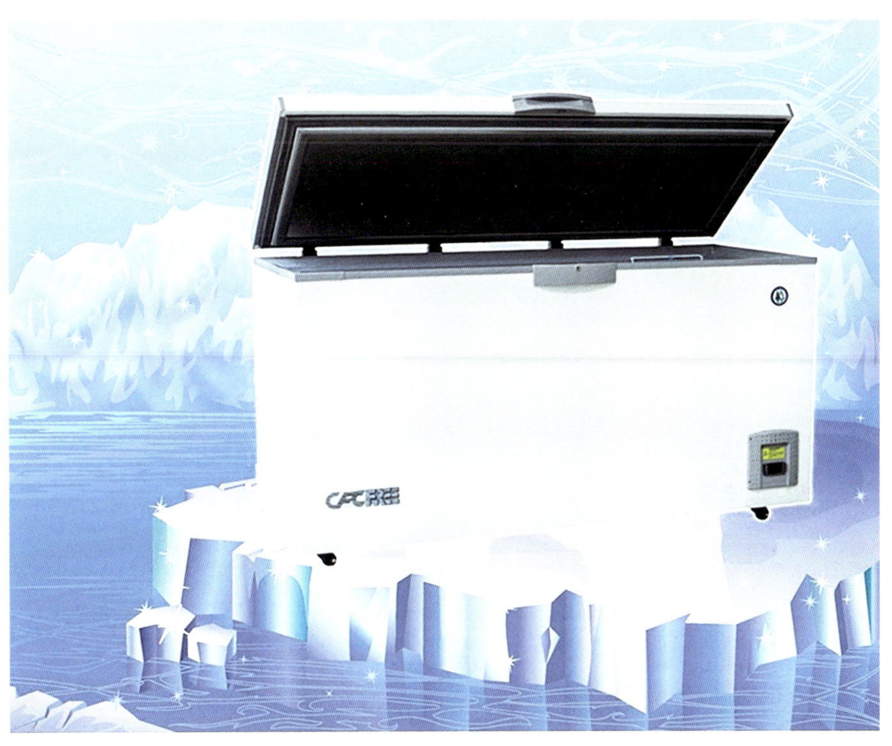

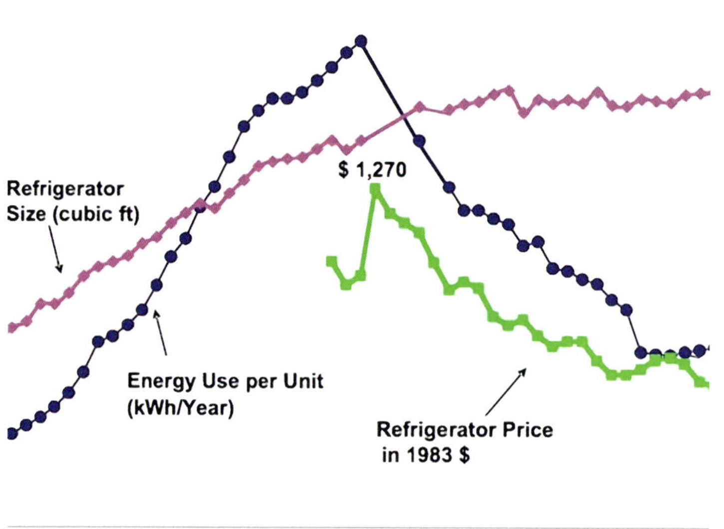

Source: David Goldstein

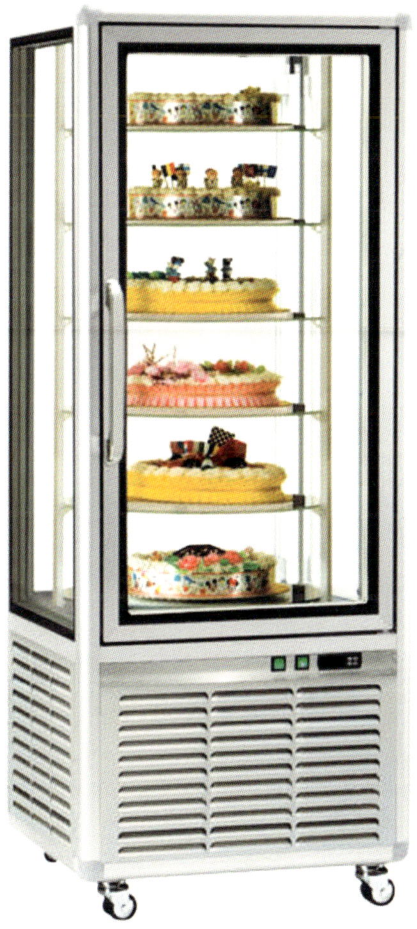

Within the universe of things, artworks occupy a special status. They are meant to be looked at and thought about, not touched and not used—transferred to the realm of *noli me tangere*. Imitating this setup, a cake in a refrigerated glass vitrine provokes desire. When exposed to the greedy impulse of desire, the cake is transferred out of this realm and back into the profane world, where it will be eaten with pleasure and digested in someone's body.

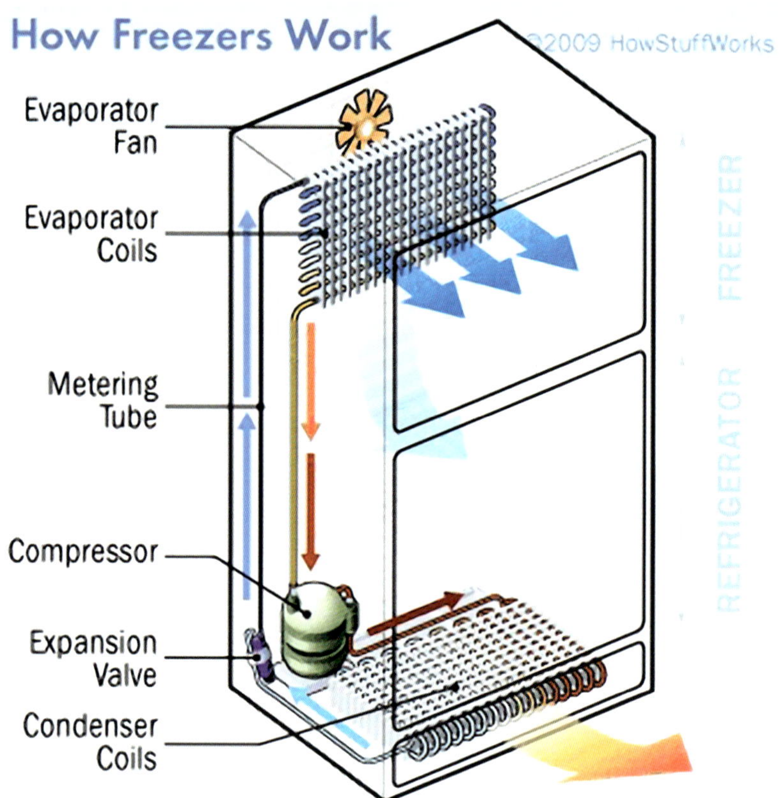
How Freezers Work
©2009 HowStuffWorks
Evaporator Fan
Evaporator Coils
Metering Tube
Compressor
Expansion Valve
Condenser Coils
FREEZER
REFRIGERATOR

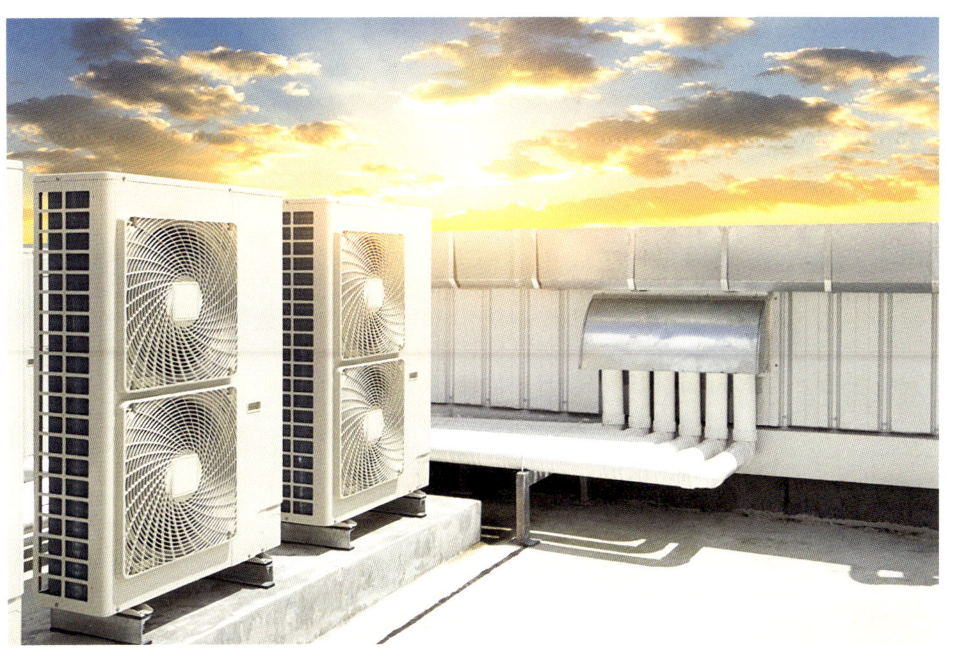

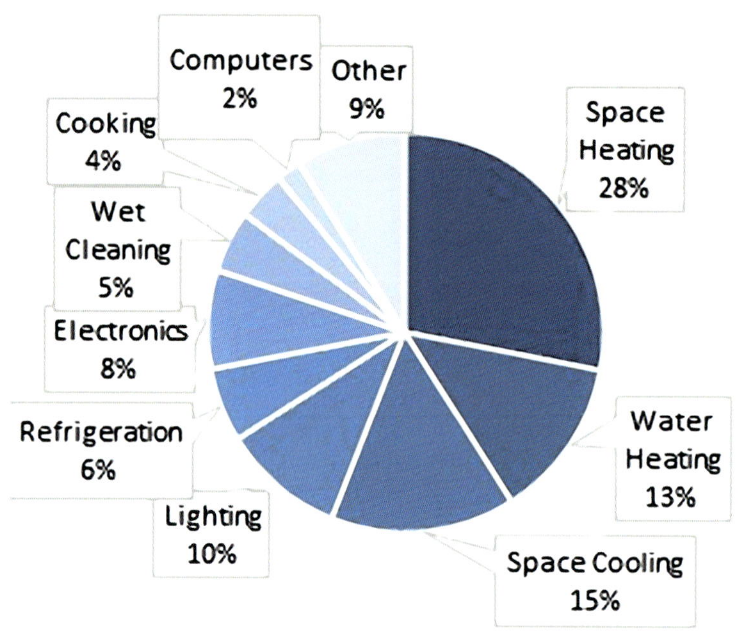
Computers
2%
Other
9%
Cooking
4%
Space
Heating
28%
Wet
Cleaning
5%
Electronics
8%
Refrigeration
6%
Water
Heating
13%
Lighting
10%
Space Cooling
15%

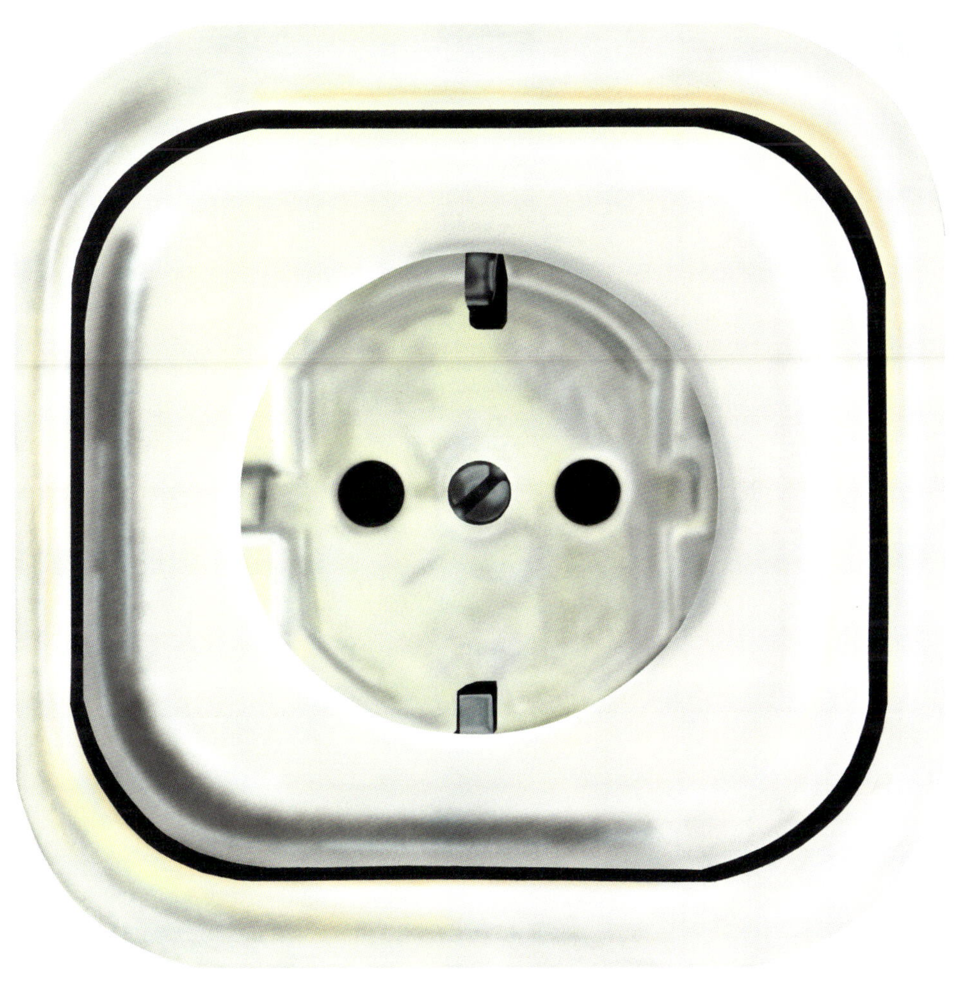

Jana Euler, *Where the Energy Comes From 1*, 2014. Acrylic on canvas

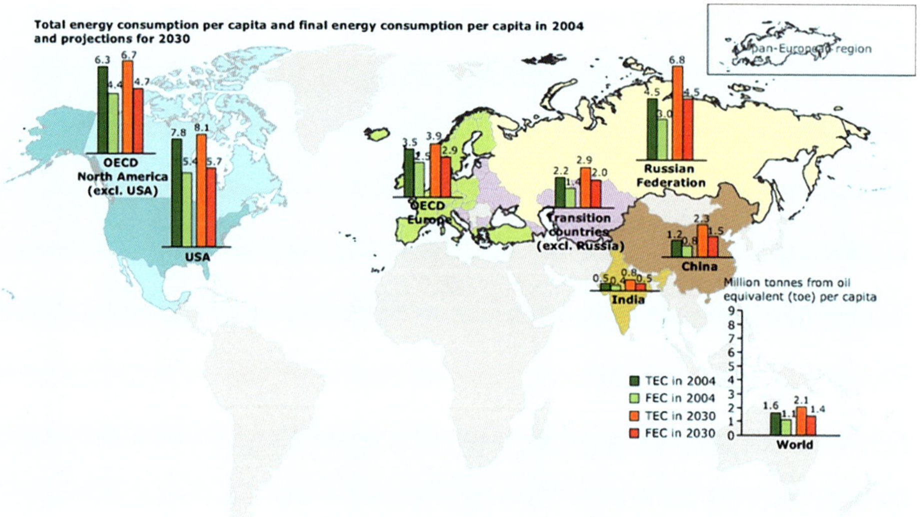
Total energy consumption per capita and final energy consumption per capita in 2004
and projections for 2030
pan-European region
6.3
4.4
6.7
4.7
OECD
North America
(excl. USA)
7.8
5.4
8.1
5.7
USA
3.5
2.5
3.9
2.9
OECD
Europe
2.2
1.4
2.9
2.0
Transition
countries
(excl. Russia)
4.5
3.0
6.8
4.5
Russian
Federation
1.2
0.8
2.3
1.5
China
0.5
0.4
0.8
0.5
India
Million tonnes from oil
equivalent (toe) per capita
TEC in 2004
FEC in 2004
TEC in 2030
FEC in 2030
1.6
1.1
2.1
1.4
World

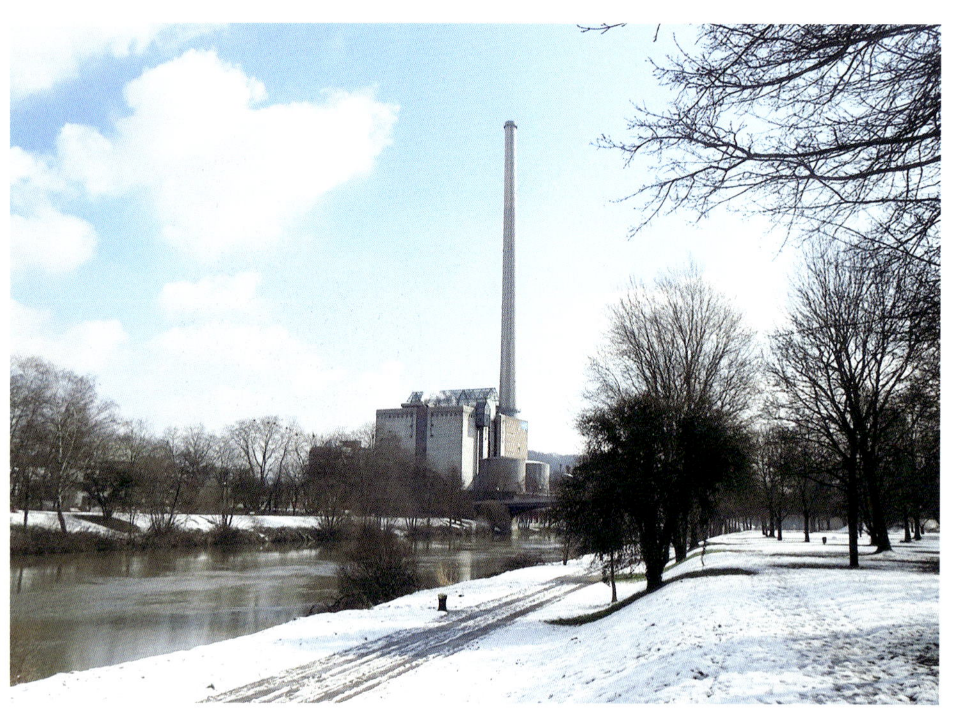

Heizkraftwerk Römerbrücke, Saarbrücken. In 1987, this site was a coal-burning plant, producing energy in the form of district heat and electricity to the citizens of the city.

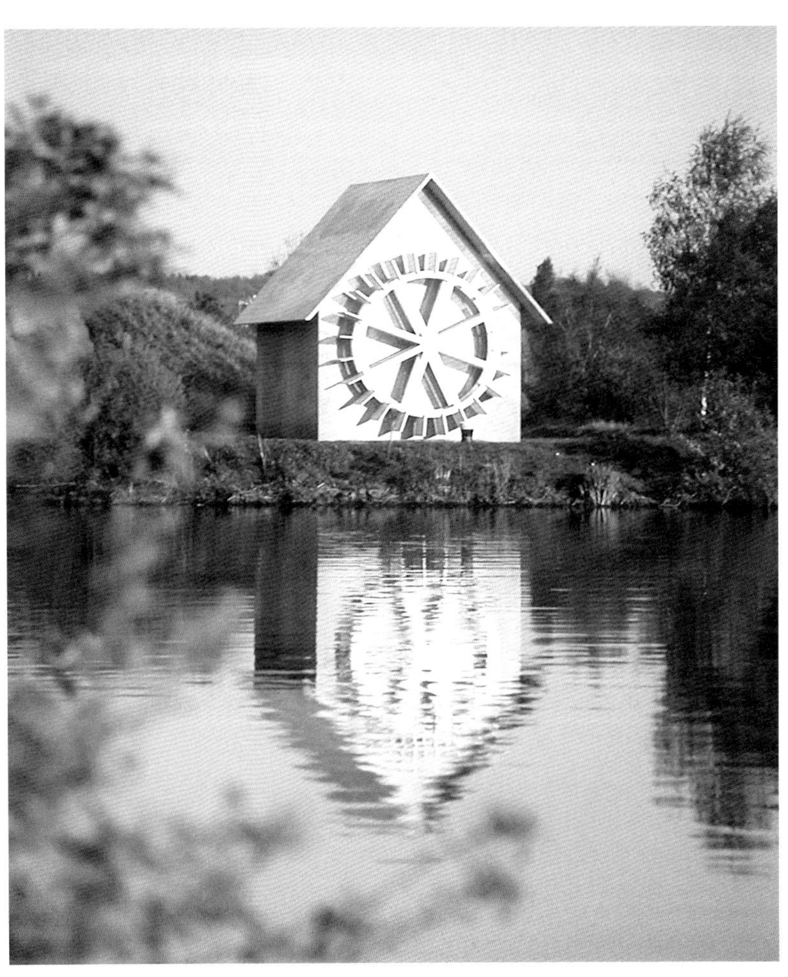

Katharina Fritsch, *Mühle*. Commission for Kunstprojekt Heizkraftwerk Römerbrücke, 1989

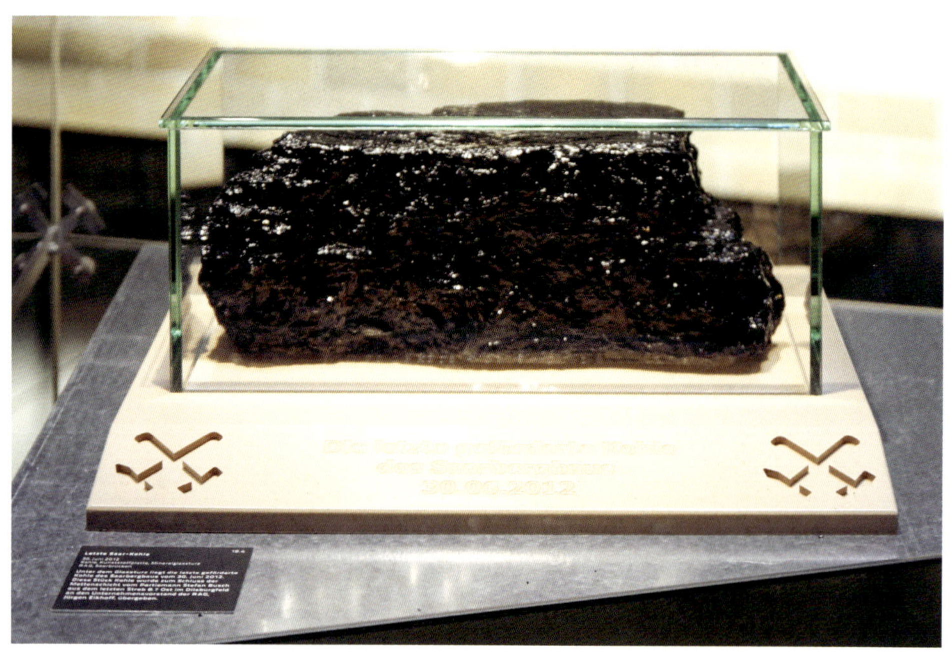

Coal was an important raw material for trading, wealth, and industry in and around Saarbrücken in the nineteenth and twentieth centuries. Coal mines proliferated in this period as emblems of progress across the German landscape. In recent years, efforts have been made to transform these coal-burning plants to gas-powered ones.
On June 30, 2012, the last piece of coal was mined in the Saarland region and preserved as an artifact in a glass vitrine.

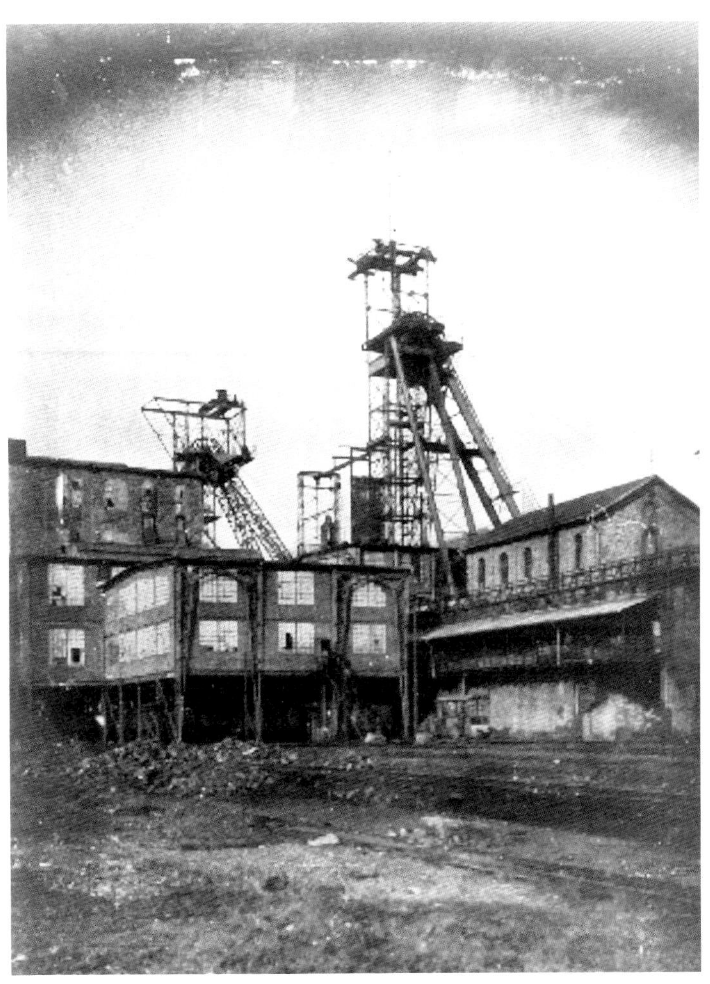

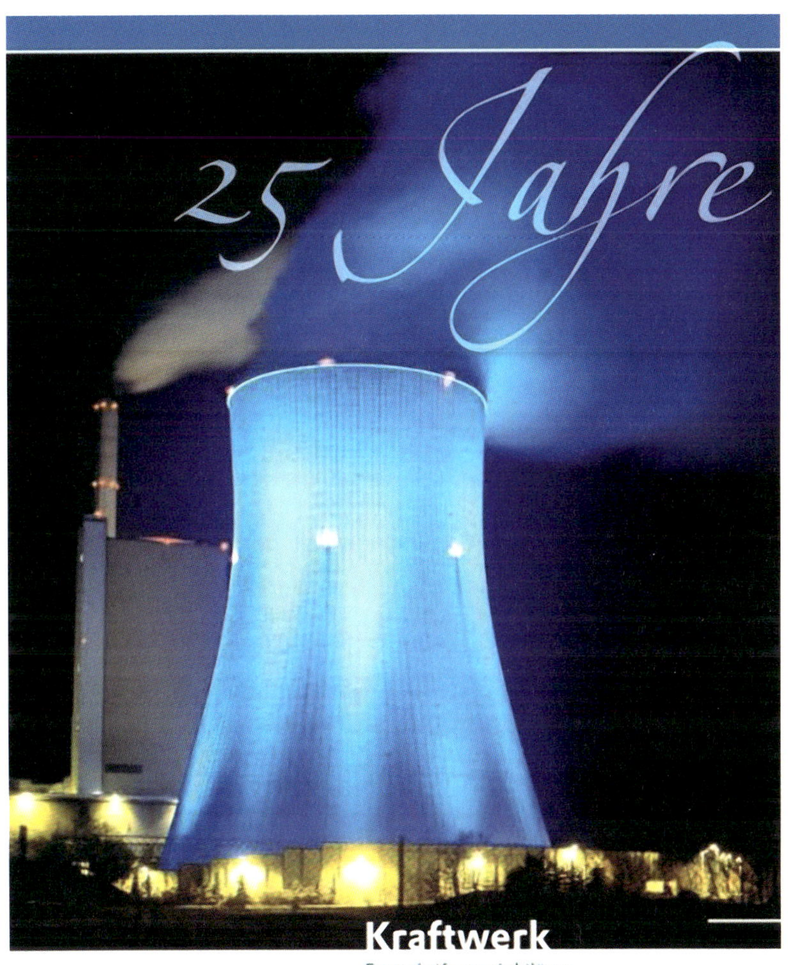

Twenty-fifth Anniversary celebration card for a power plant

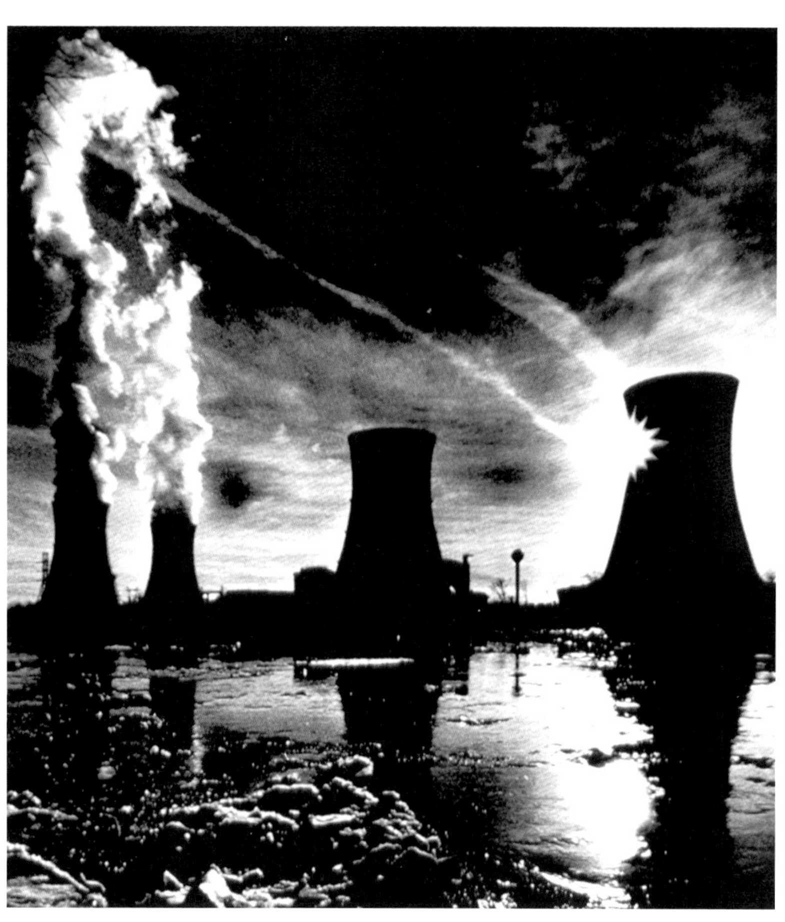

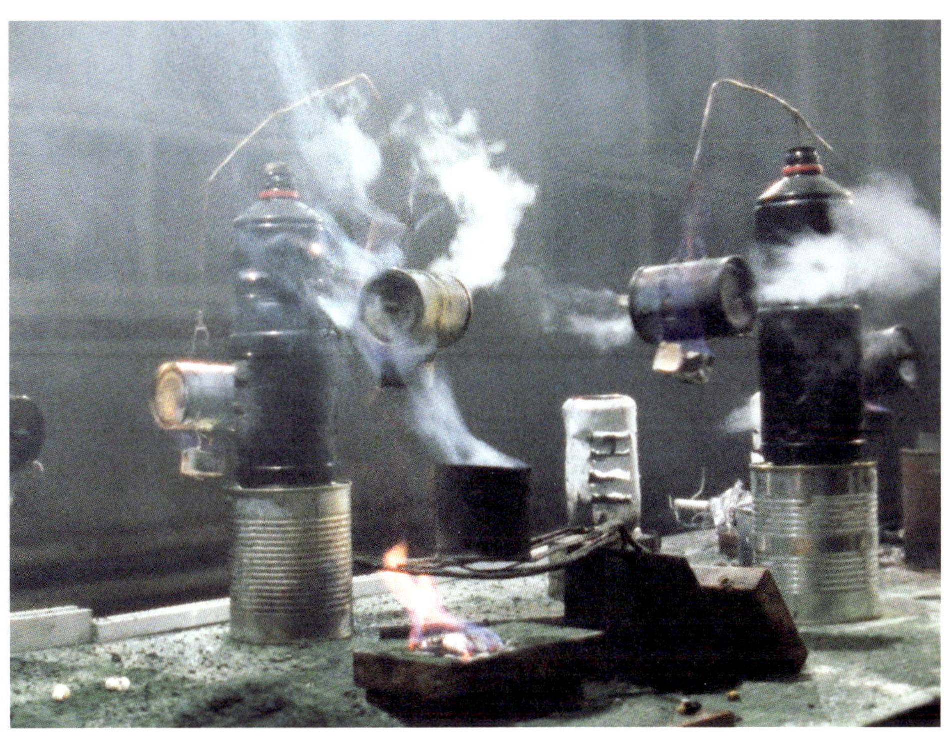

The Way Things Go documents a long causal chain of actions precipitated by objects. This particular scene was given the studio title "Kraftwerk." The invitation to make an artwork for a powerplant arrived in the artists' studio in 1987, months after the nuclear catastrophe at Chernobyl. Fischli/Weiss, still from *The Way Things Go*, 1987. 16 mm, 30 min

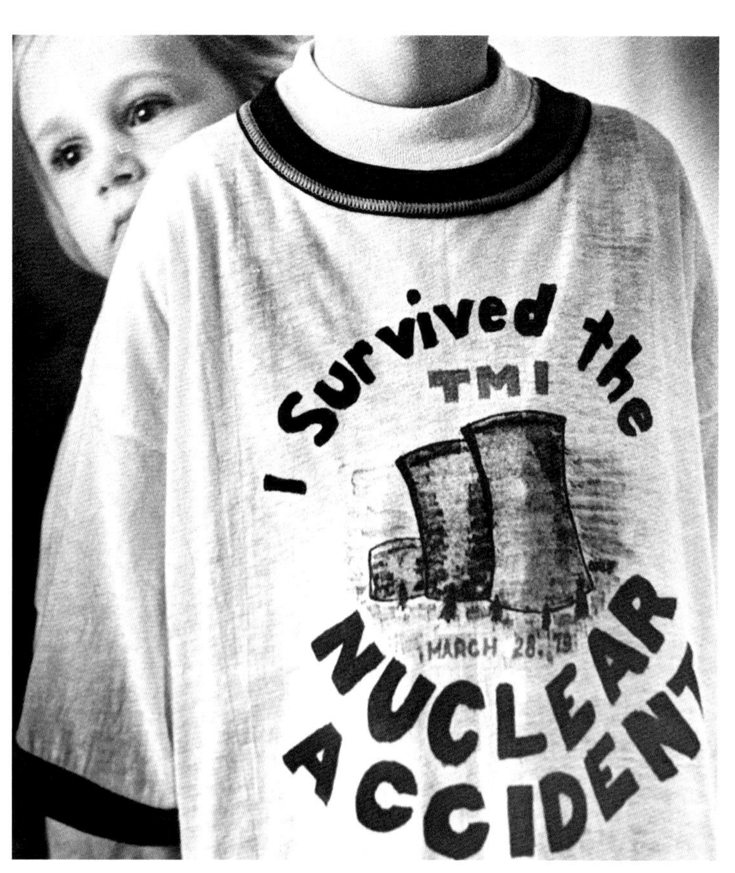
I Survived the
TMI
MARCH 28, 79
NUCLEAR
ACCIDENT

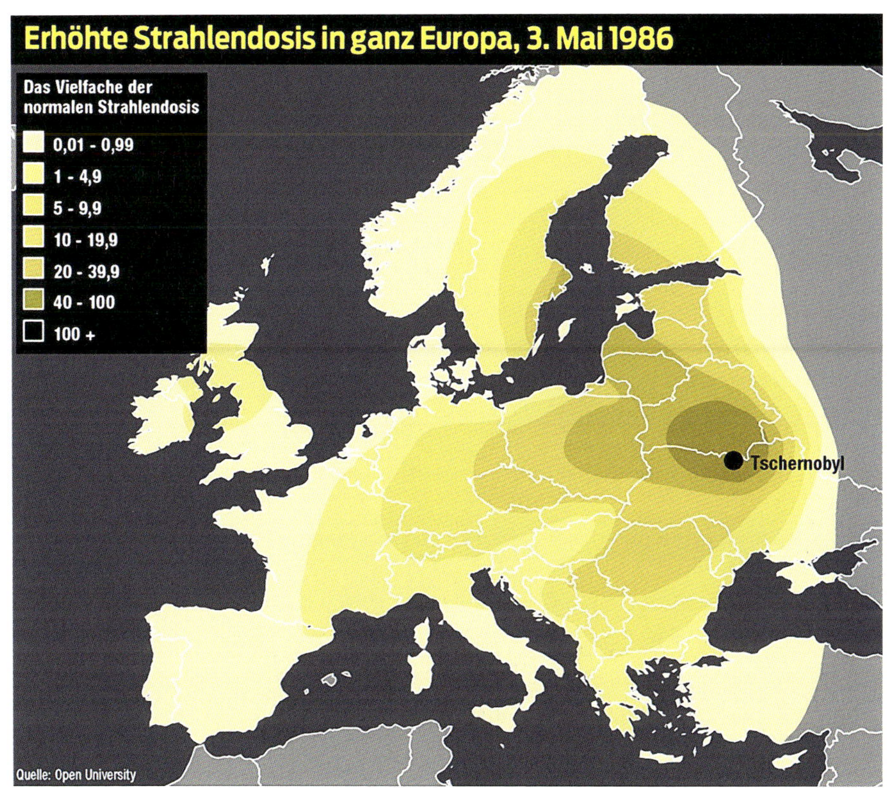

Map of radiation levels across Europe, May 3, 1986

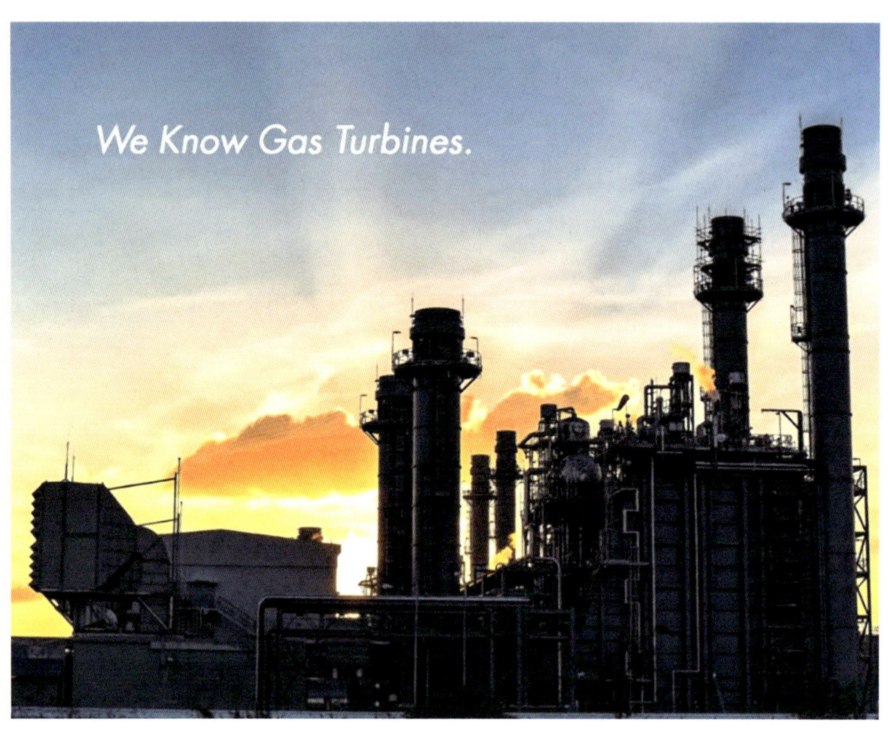

In 2020, the Heizkraftwerk Römerbrücke began a major renovation effort to completely phase out coal fuel, and its inauguration was a public affair. According to a public relations text posted at the construction site published by the plant's operator, Energie SaarLorLux, the project was expected to be completed by April 2022.

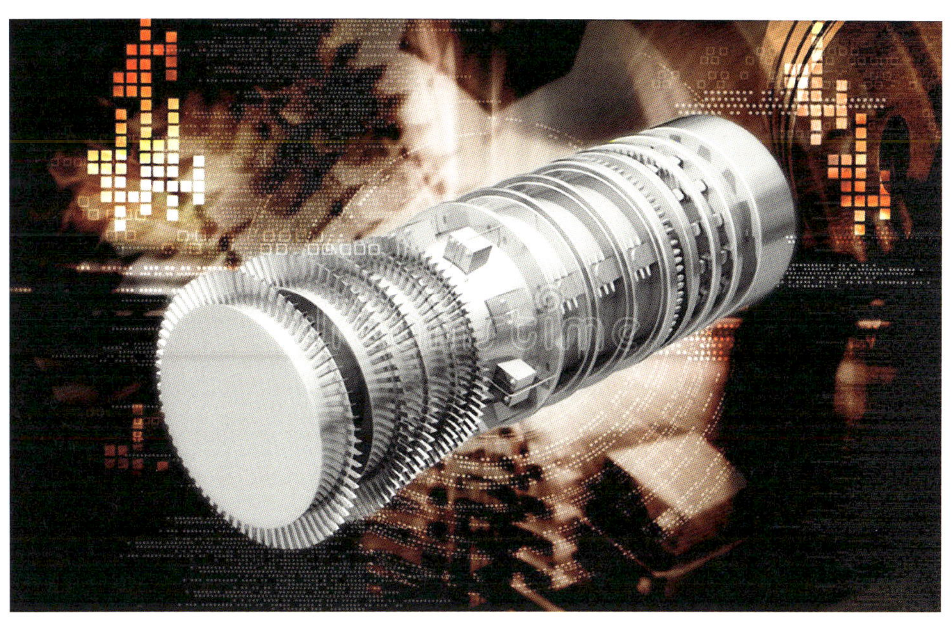

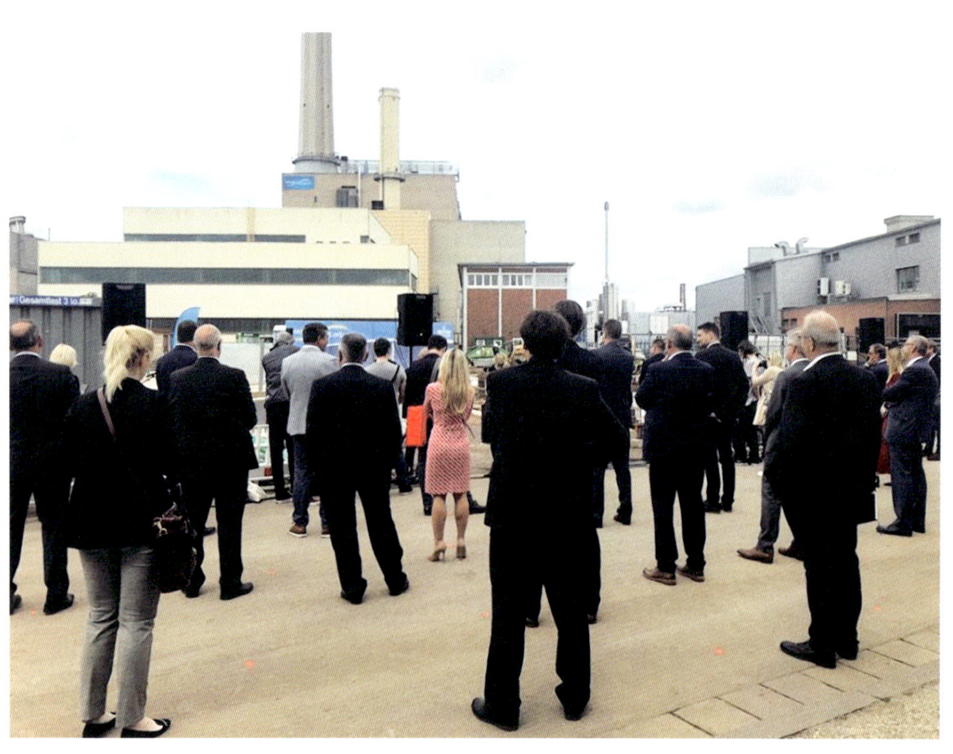

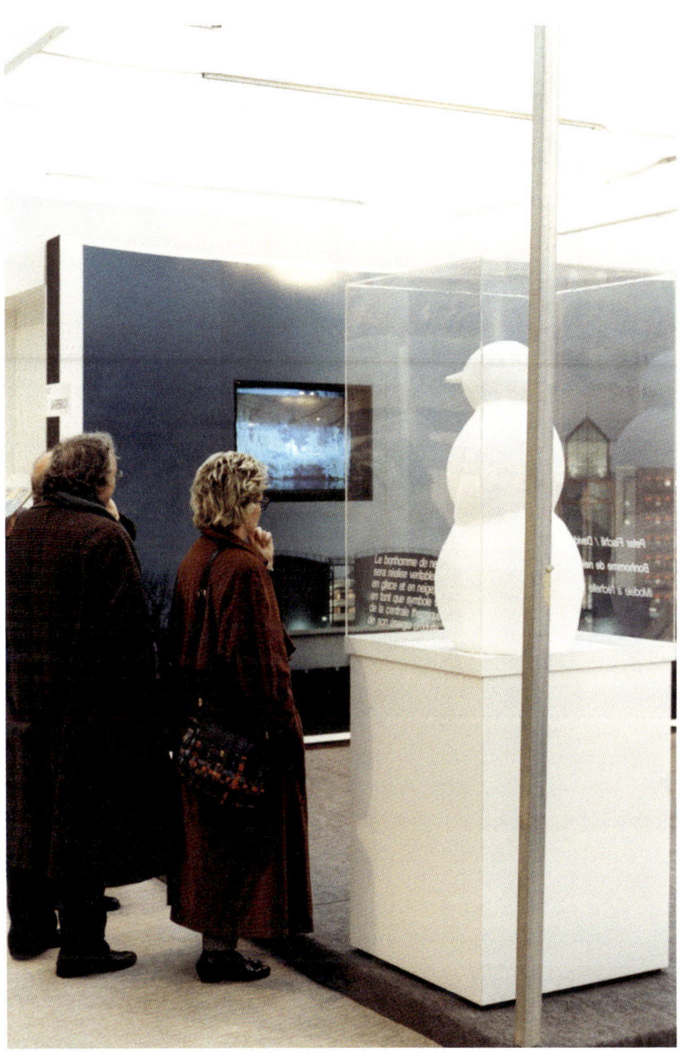

A model for *Snowman* was displayed in a public exposition that presented an architectural project and related artwork commissions at Heizkraftwerk Römerbrücke to the people of Saarbrücken. Fischli/Weiss, model for *Snowman*, 1988. Painted polyurethane

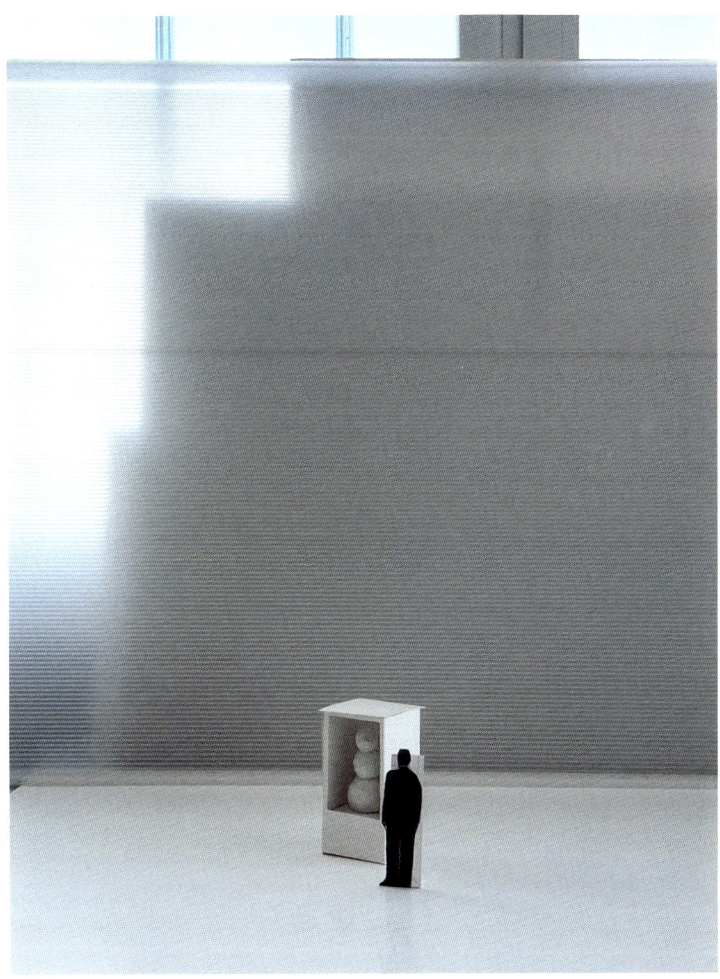

Reconstruction of cardboard model for *Snowman*, sited in front of the powerplant's main building

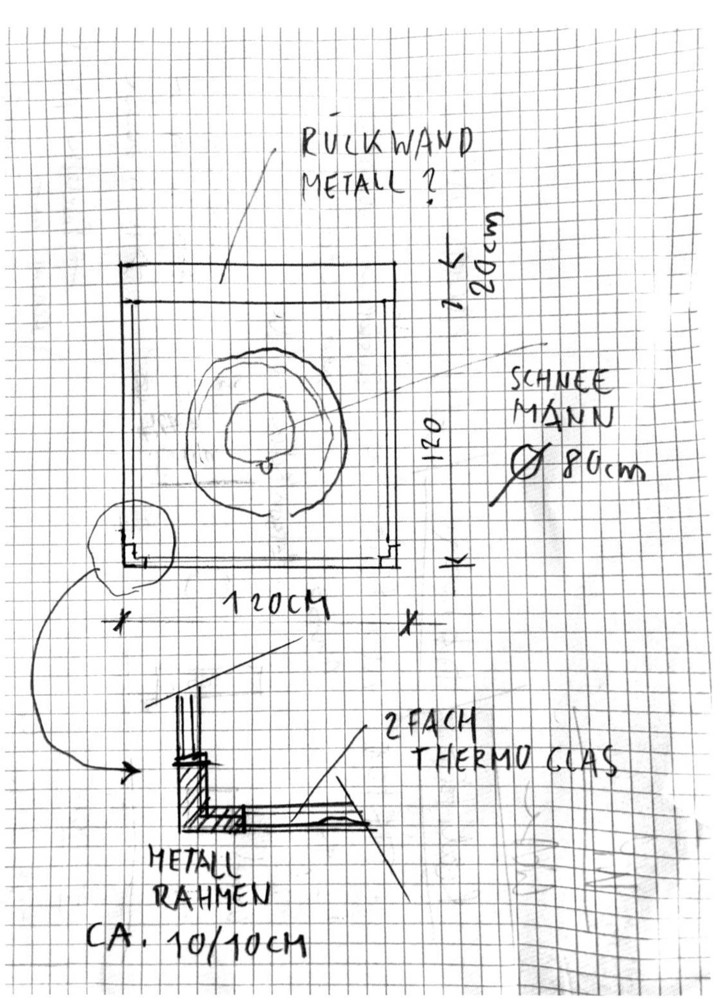

Sketch for *Snowman* vitrine, 1987

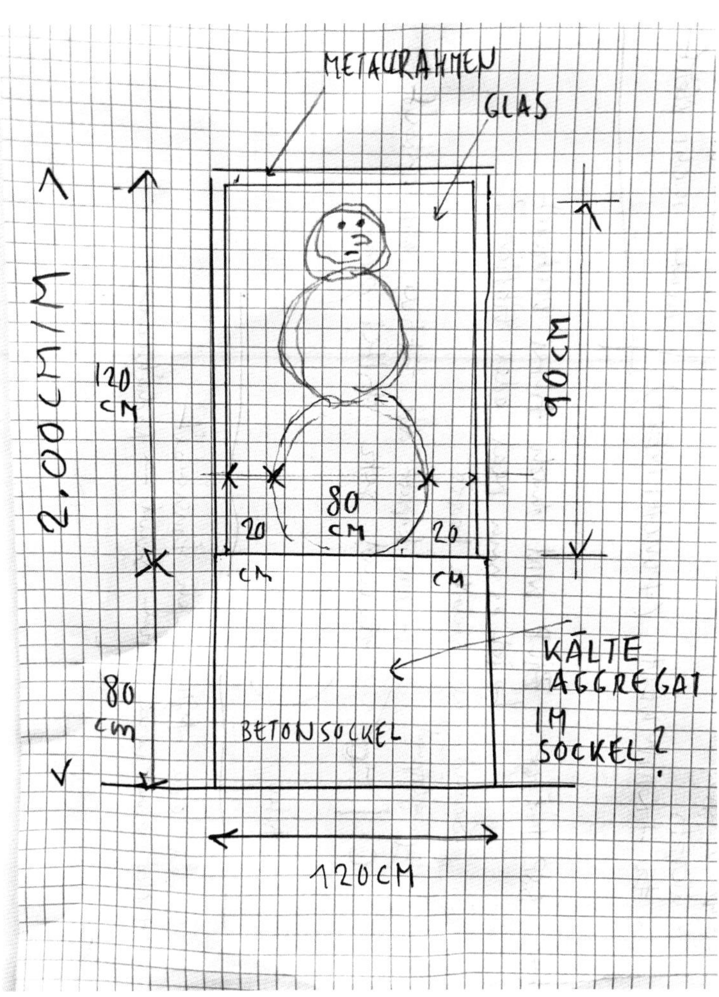
METALLRAHMEN
GLAS
2,00 CM/M
120 CM
90CM
20 CM
80 CM
20 CM
80 cm
BETONSOCKEL
KÄLTE AGGREGAT IM SOCKEL ?
120CM

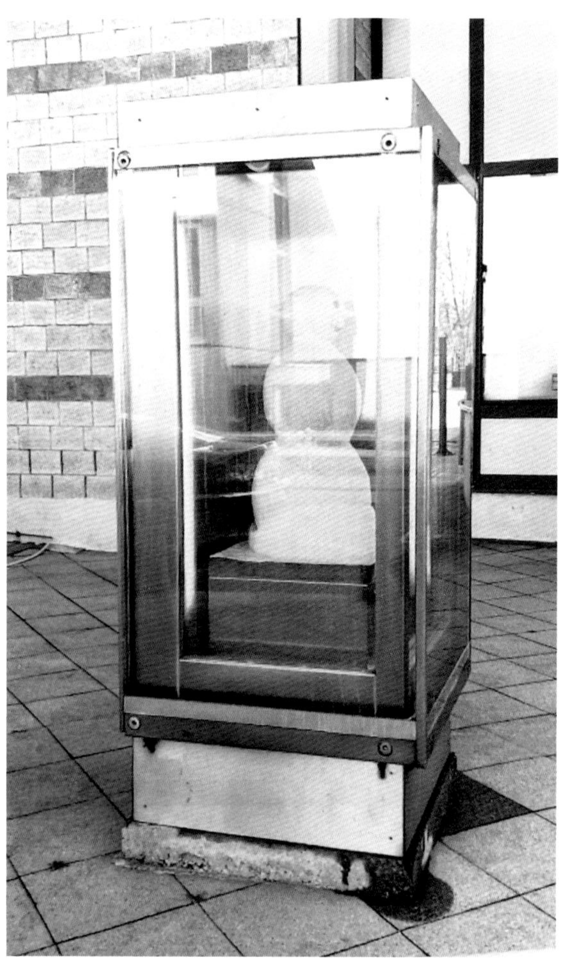

Snowman was positioned next to the porter's lodge at the entryway to the Heizkraftwerk Römerbrücke, where it played the informal role of the plant's gatekeeper or "mascot." It was the hope that the porter would have the keys to the vitrine and would assume the responsibility of the work's caretaker, controlling the temperature in the freezer to keep the amount of built-up snow consistent, and manually adjusting the snowman's form as necessary. Fischli/Weiss, *Snowman*, 1987. Copper, stainless steel, glass, water, and coolant system

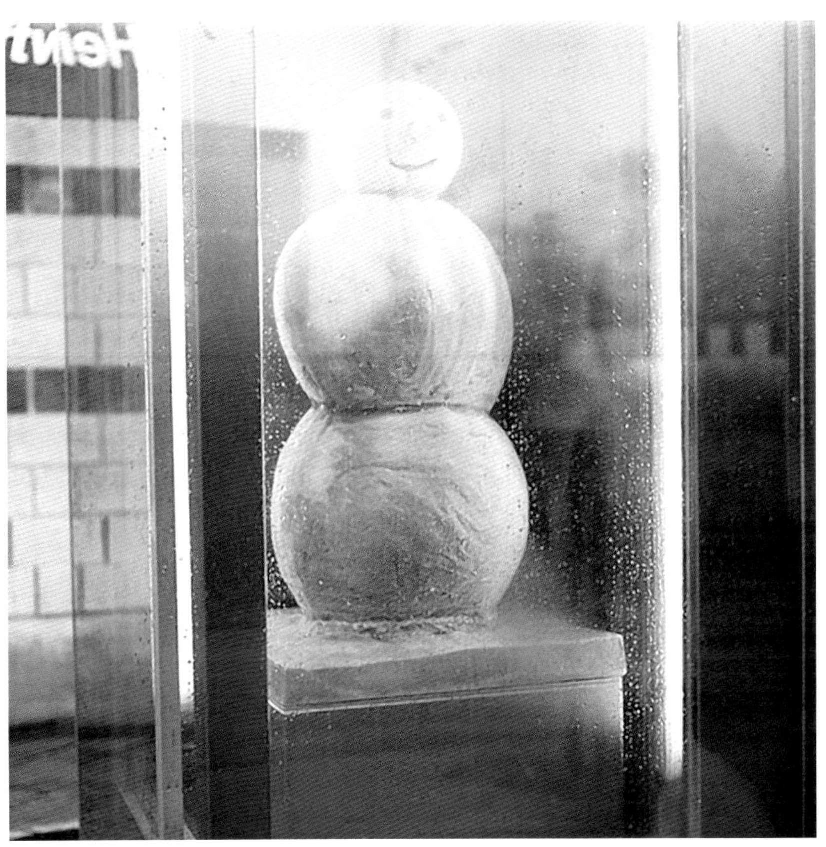

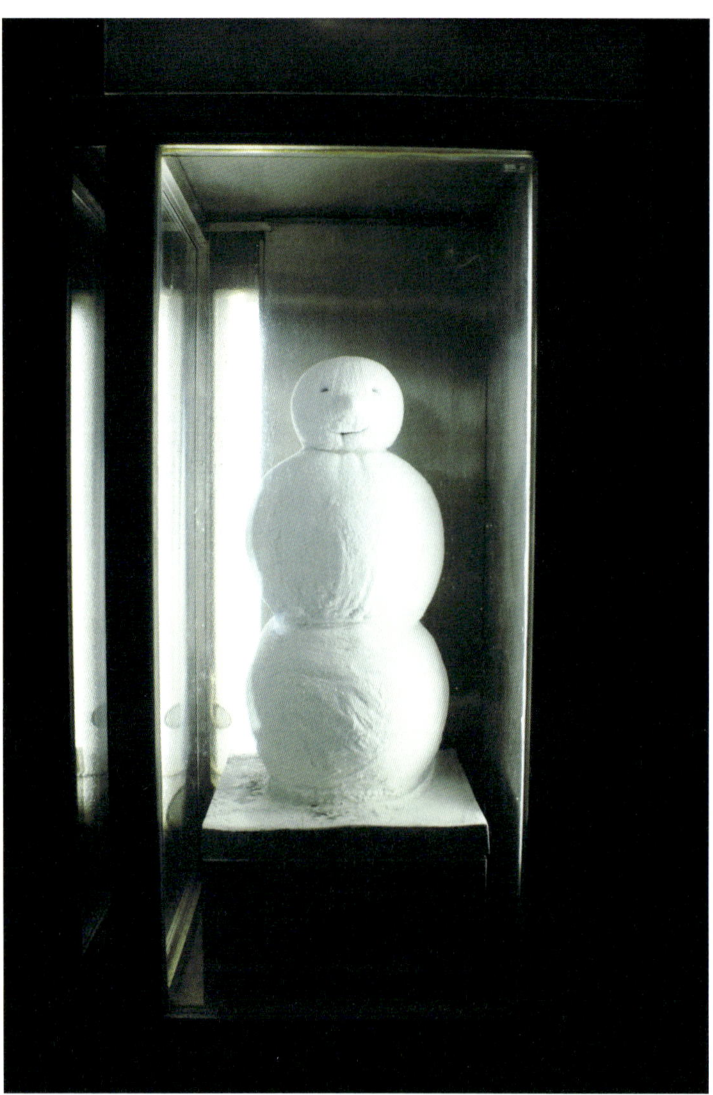

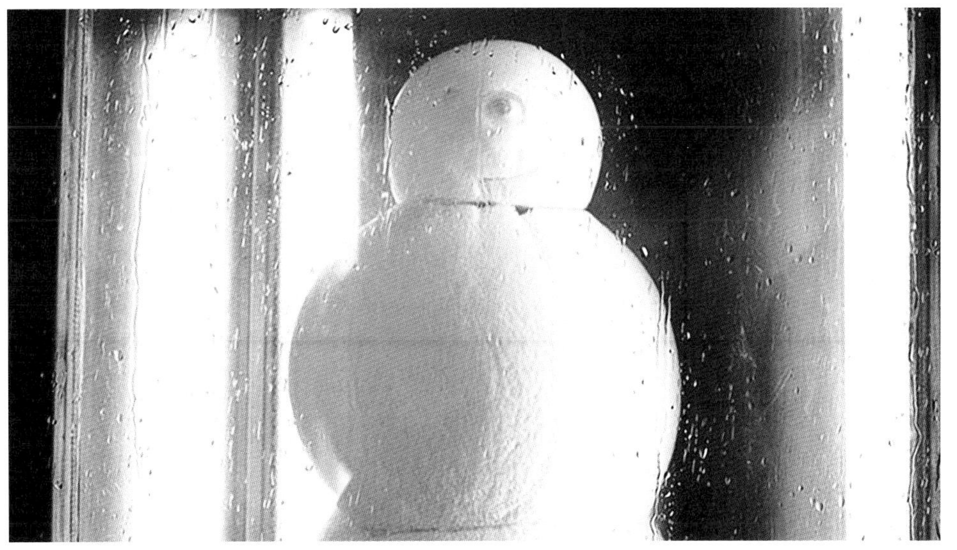

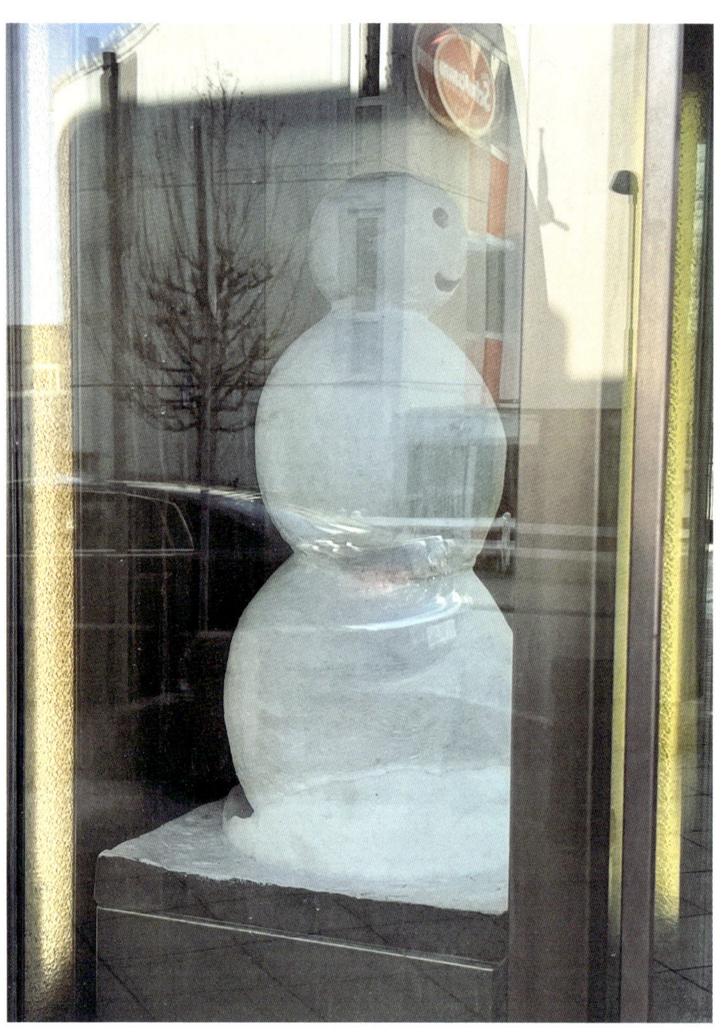

„Schneemann"

Kunstwerk von Peter Fischli und David Weiss

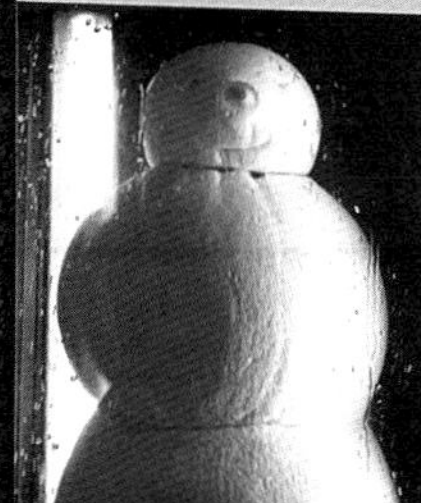

In der tiefgekühlten Vitrine empfängt der Schneemann die Besucher des Kraftwerks.

Die Schweizer Fischli und Weiss haben das Kunstwerk so konzipiert, dass der kugelige Grundkörper nur dann mit einer Raureifschicht überzogen ist, wenn Strom im Heizkraftwerk produziert wird. Der Gegensatz von Eis (beim Schneemann) und Feuer (für die Stromerzeugung) ist für die Künstler ein „sehr starker Kommentar über den Ort".

Beim Betrieb des Heizkraftwerks Römerbrücke ist es nichts Ungewöhnliches, wenn der Schneemann zeitweise abgetaut ist. Dies kann z. B. während Revisions- und Wartungsphasen der Fall sein, oder im Sommer, wenn weniger Strom benötigt wird.

Das Heizkraftwerk ist dann aber trotzdem in Betrieb und erzeugt umweltfreundliche Fernwärme für Saarbrücken.

Unabhängig von der jeweiligen Betriebsweise des Heizkraftwerks garantieren wir als Energie SaarLorLux die Versorgungssicherheit stets – so, wie unsere Kunden das von uns in den vergangenen Jahrzehnten gewohnt sind.

The Heizkraftwerk Römerbrücke made the decision, for energy conservation reasons, to power off *Snowman* during the summer months, when heat production is low. As a justification for that decision, the plant installed an explanatory panel near the artwork.

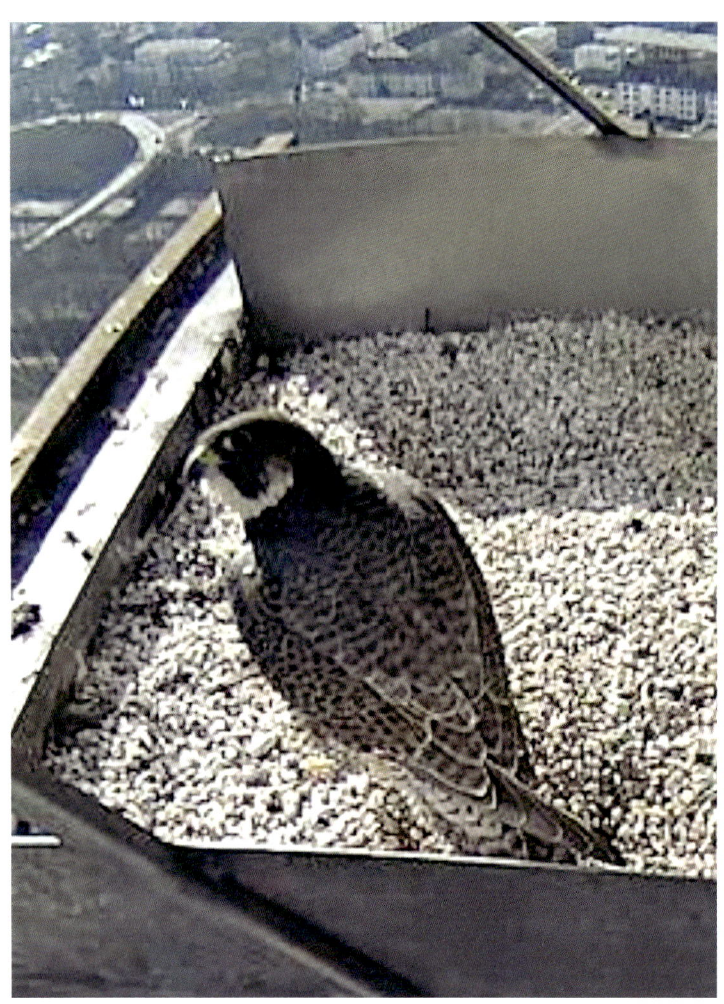

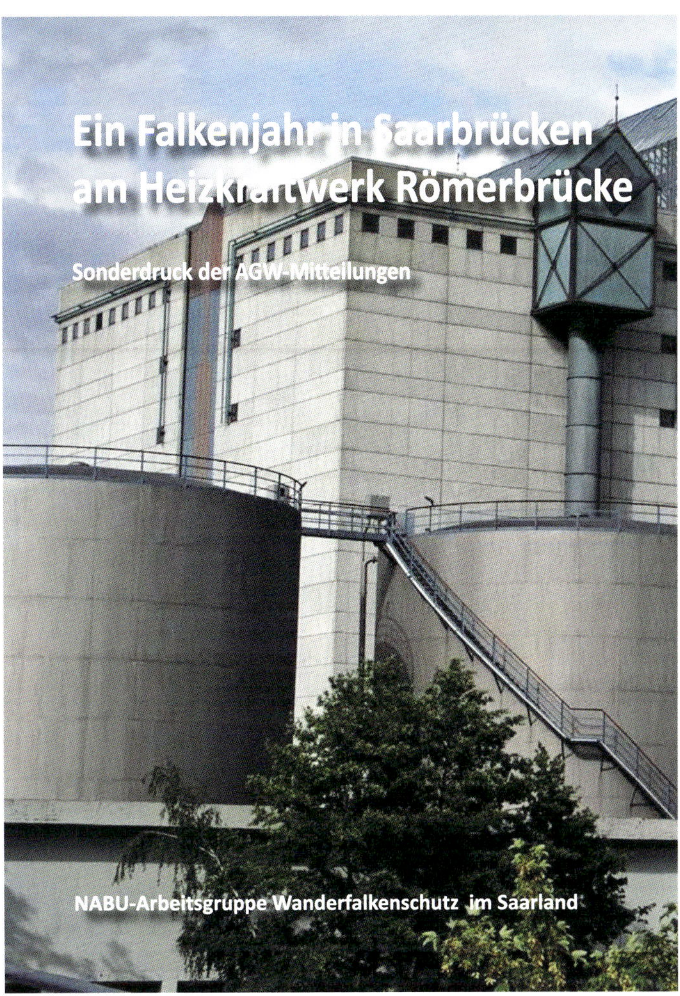

Returning to the topic of the "mascot," years later, coincidentally, a pair of peregrine falcons, Heinz and Hilde, took up a nest on the smokestack of the Heizkraftwerk Römerbrücke. Now the people of Saarbrücken can observe the birds' activities via a webcam installed near their nest, twenty-four hours a day, seven days a week.

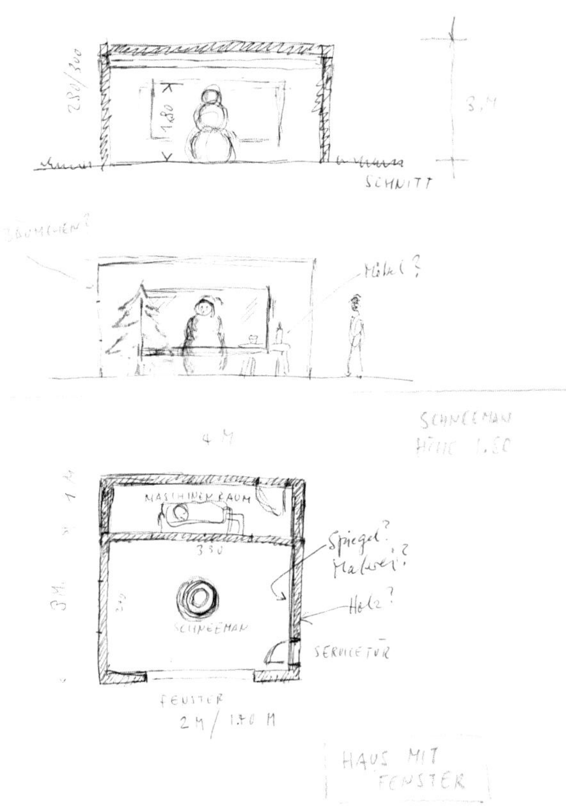

In 2008, Philippe Vergne, then director of the Walker Art Center, expressed interest in presenting *Snowman* in the Walker's sculpture garden. The invitation encouraged Fischli/Weiss to reconfigure the technical and aesthetic aspects of the sculpture. The first attempts to do so involved placing the snowman inside of a large, horizontal vitrine, which could potentially accommodate a tree and select furniture. Investigations were conducted into the feasibility of producing a freezer that could house a domestic tableau, as opposed to a solo object. Sketches, model, planning, and construction documents for a possible presentation of *Snowman* at Walker Art Center, Minneapolis

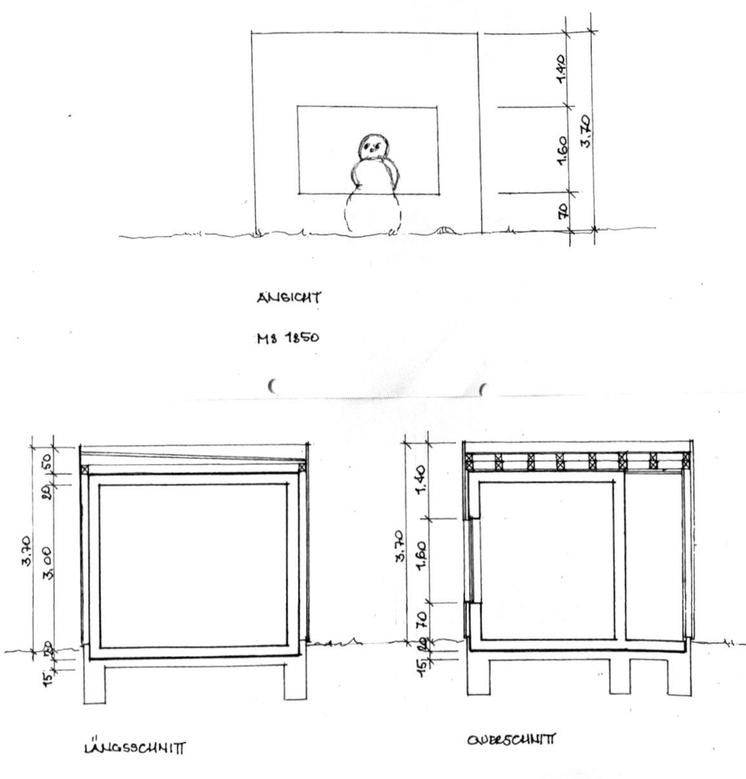

1.40
1.60
3.70
70
ANSICHT
MS 1:50
50
20
3.70
3.00
15
LÄNGSSCHNITT
MS 1:50
1.40
3.70
1.60
70
15
QUERSCHNITT

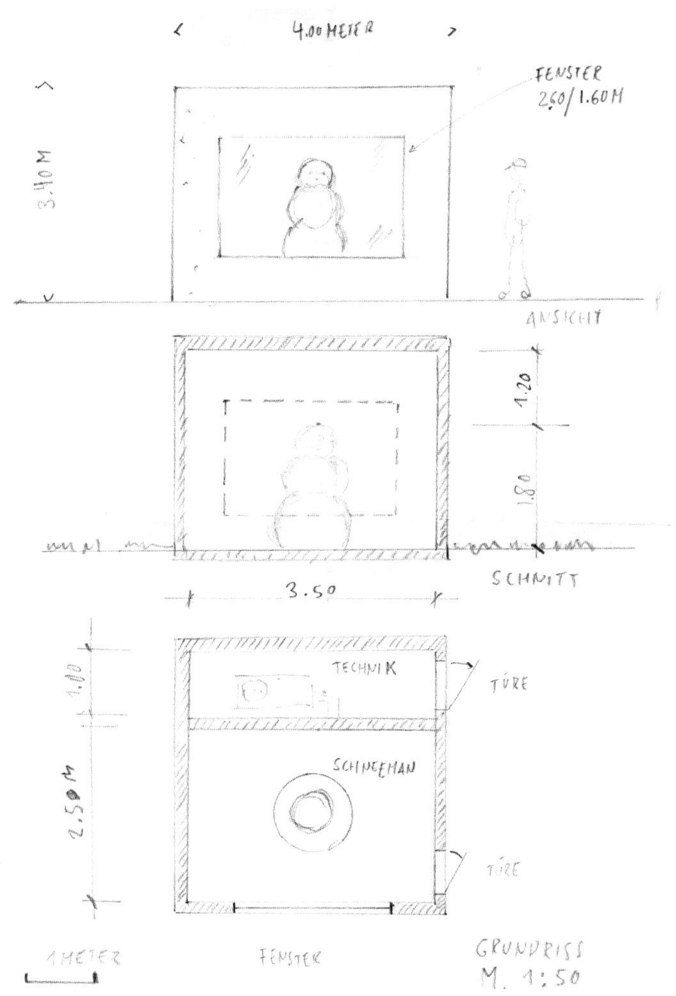
4.00 METER
FENSTER
2,60/1.60M
3.40M
ANSICHT
1.20
1.80
SCHNITT
3.50
TECHNIK
TÜRE
1.00
SCHNEEMAN
2.50M
TÜRE
1 METER
FENSTER
GRUNDRISS
M. 1:50

Eventually, the idea to build a small house for the snowman was abandoned in favor of a vitrine-like aluminum sculpture as a container. The project remained unrealized for the Walker Art Center, but these designs served as the blueprint for the version that was ultimately fabricated in 2016.

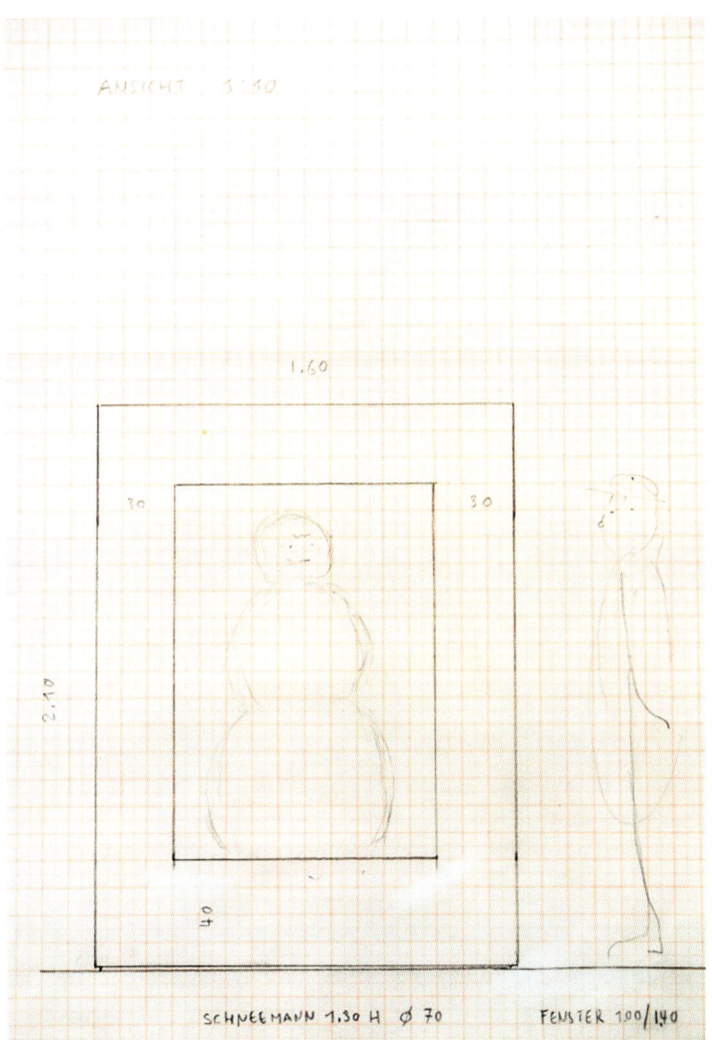
ANSICHT 1:10
1.60
30
30
2.10
40
SCHNEEMANN 1.30 H Ø 70
FENSTER 1,00/1,40

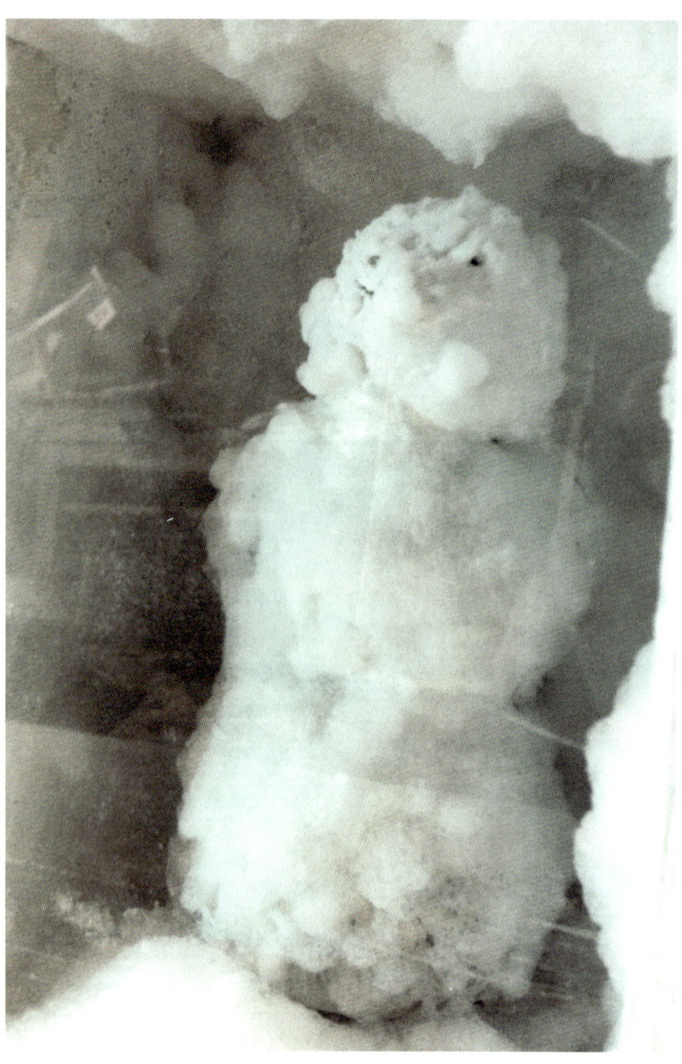

During the planning phases for the Walker Art Center project, the idea to move away from a classical three-ball composition was discussed. A set of studies were then made for a more formless snowman.

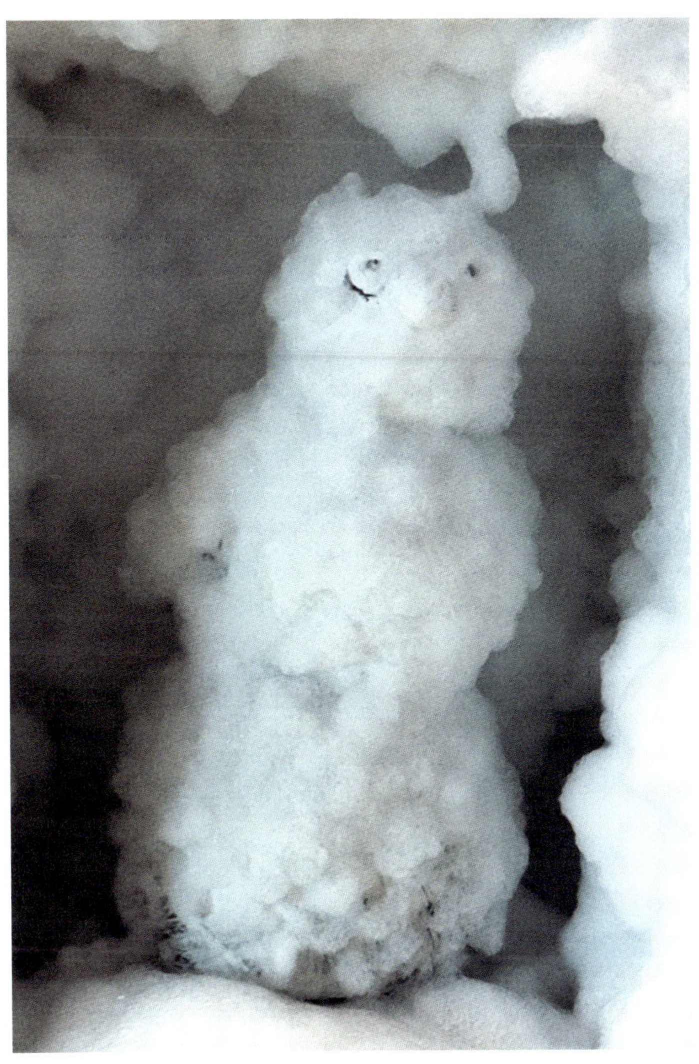

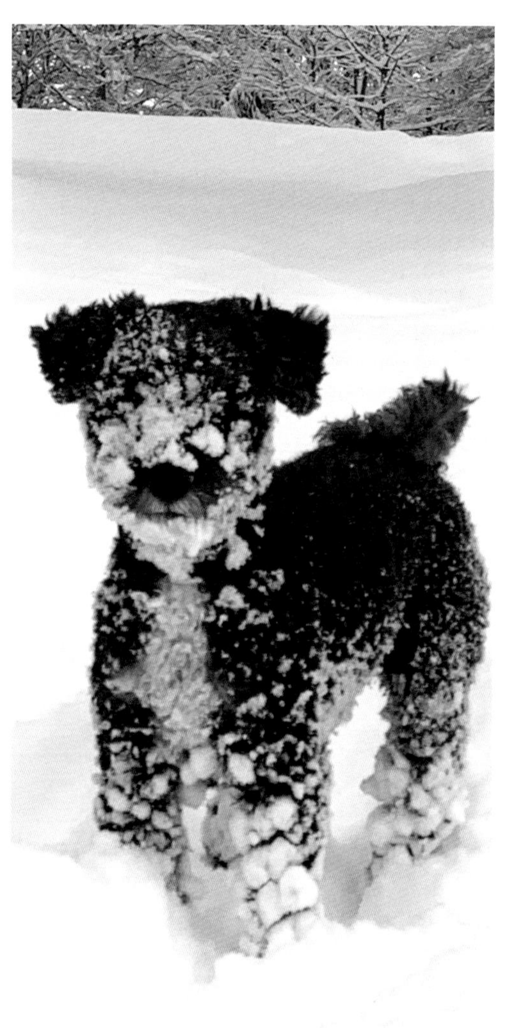

Jimmy in the snow

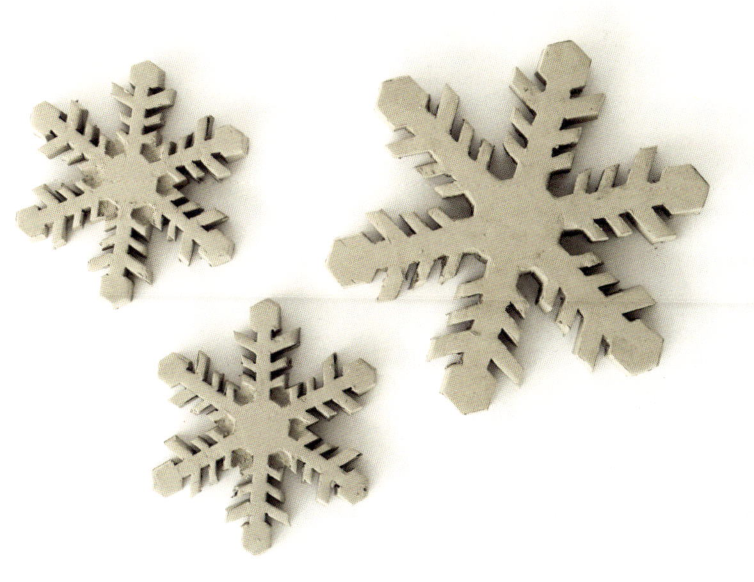

Suddenly This Overview is a group of more than 350 hand modelled, unfired clay sculptures made between 1981 and 2012 that depict scenes, objects, and phenomena from history, culture, and daily life. A subset of the group is devoted to the concept of "popular opposites." Fischli / Weiss, *Christmas Decorations*, from *Suddenly This Overview*, 1981–2012. Unfired clay

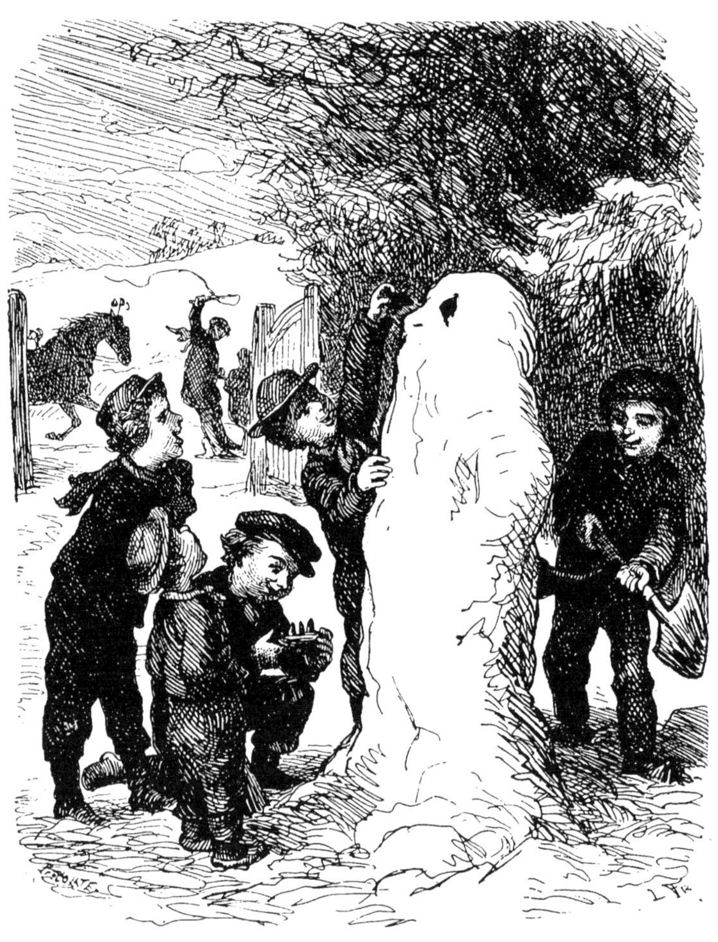

“He had been born amid the triumphant shouts of the boys,” wrote Hans Christian Andersen in 1861, “and welcomed by the jingling of sleigh bells and the cracking of whips from the passing sleighs.” Illustration by Lorenz Frølich from *The Snowman*, in Hans Christian Andersen, *Nye Eventyr og Historier II* (Copenhagen: C. A. Reitzels Forlag, 1871).

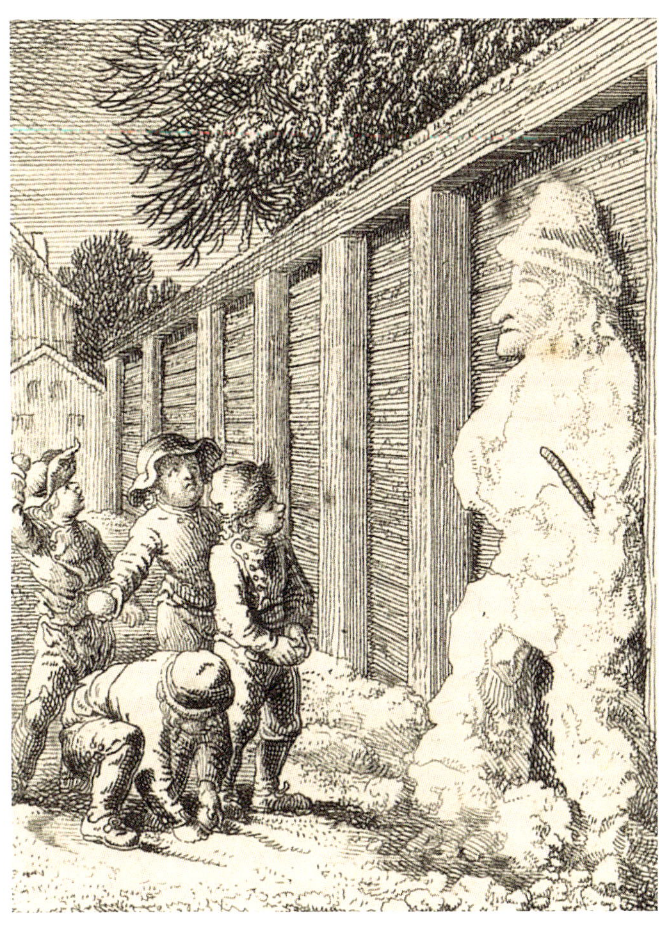

A German painter and printmaker of Polish ancestry, Daniel Chodowiecki (1726–1801) was best known for producing a body of several thousand etchings that detail the life of the bourgeoisie in the late eighteenth century. It has been suggested that this print is one of the oldest recorded renderings of a snowman. Daniel Chodowiecki, *December*, 1777. Etching, Rijksmuseum, Amsterdam

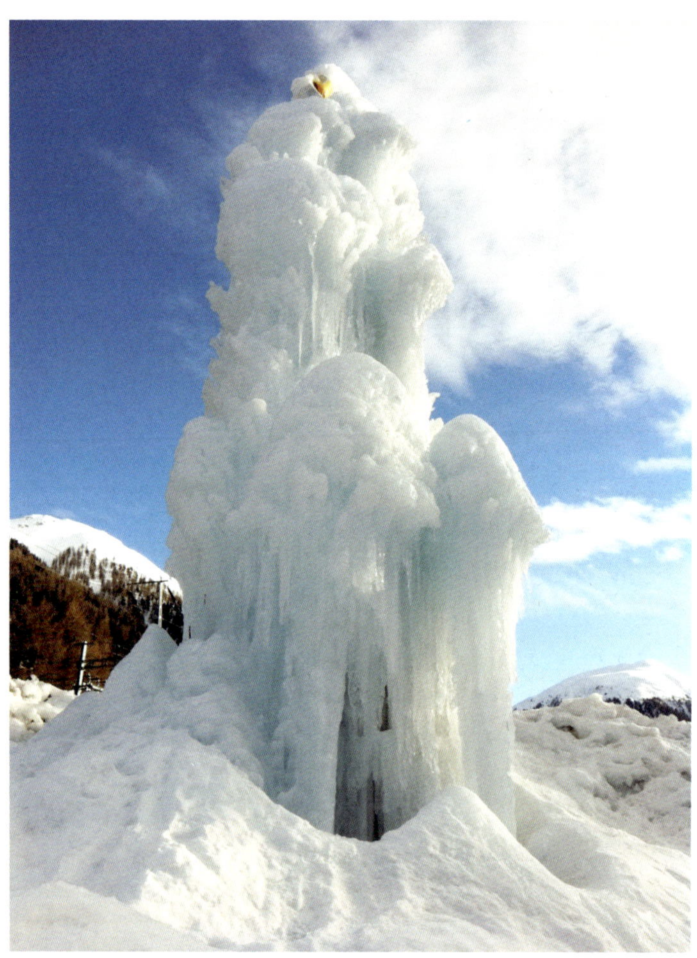

Created through an uncontrolled process of water freezing in real time, accidental ice sculptures occupy an aesthetic territory that could be described as *Ungestalt*—the antithesis of form. In German fairy tales and sagas, the *Ungestalt* is often personified by a ghost or monster from the realm of the uncanny.

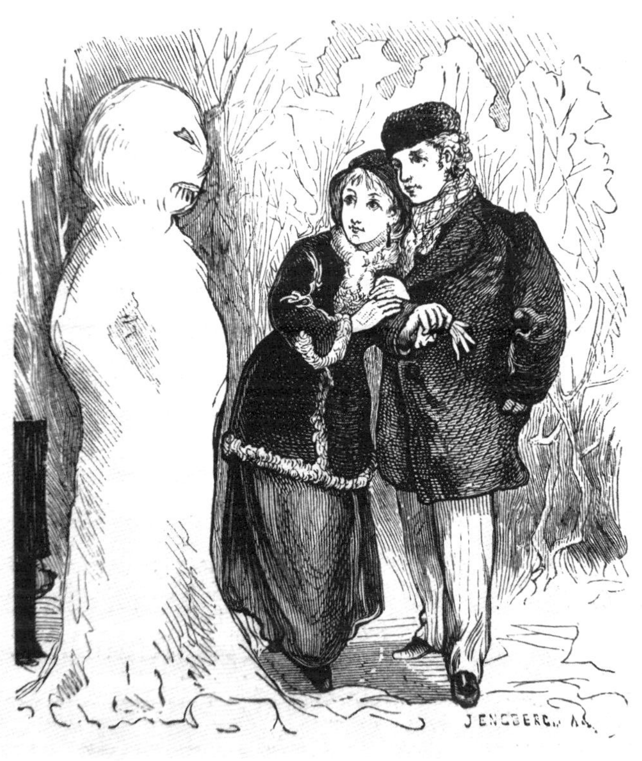

"'And we can't have such a fellow as this in the summertime,' replied the young man, pointing to the Snow Man; 'he is capital.'" Before mass industrialization and domestic heating systems became commonplace, the snowman was often considered to be a frightening figure—a reminder of winter's cruel effects. Illustration by J. Engberg from *The Snowman*, in Hans Christian Andersen, *Märchen für Kinder* (Stuttgart: Loewes Verlag, ca. 1905).

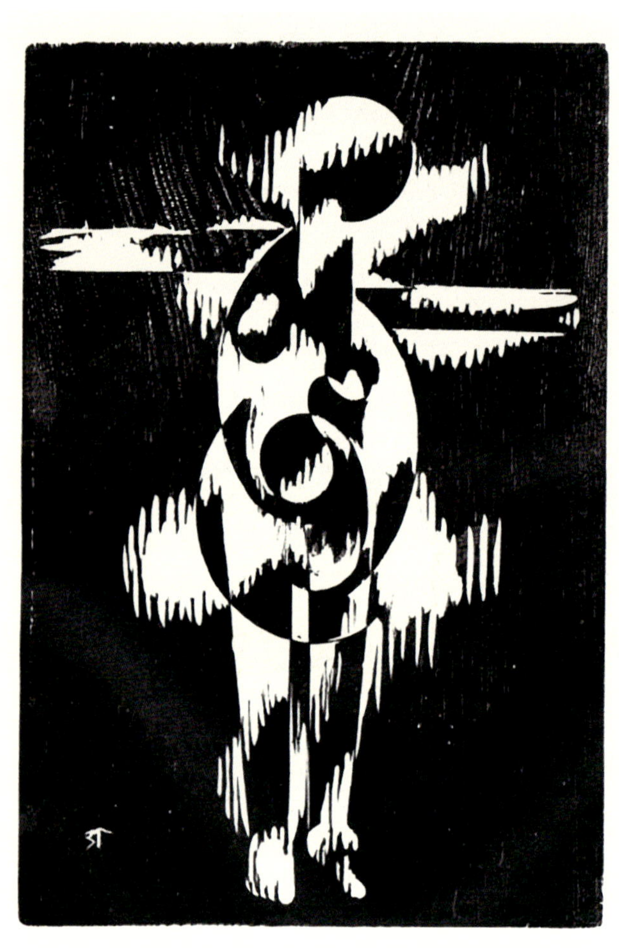

Thomas Ring, *Harmonie/Gestalt*, 1921. Woodcut for *Kündung* (1921, no. 11/12), a German Expressionist arts and literature journal published in Hamburg in 1921

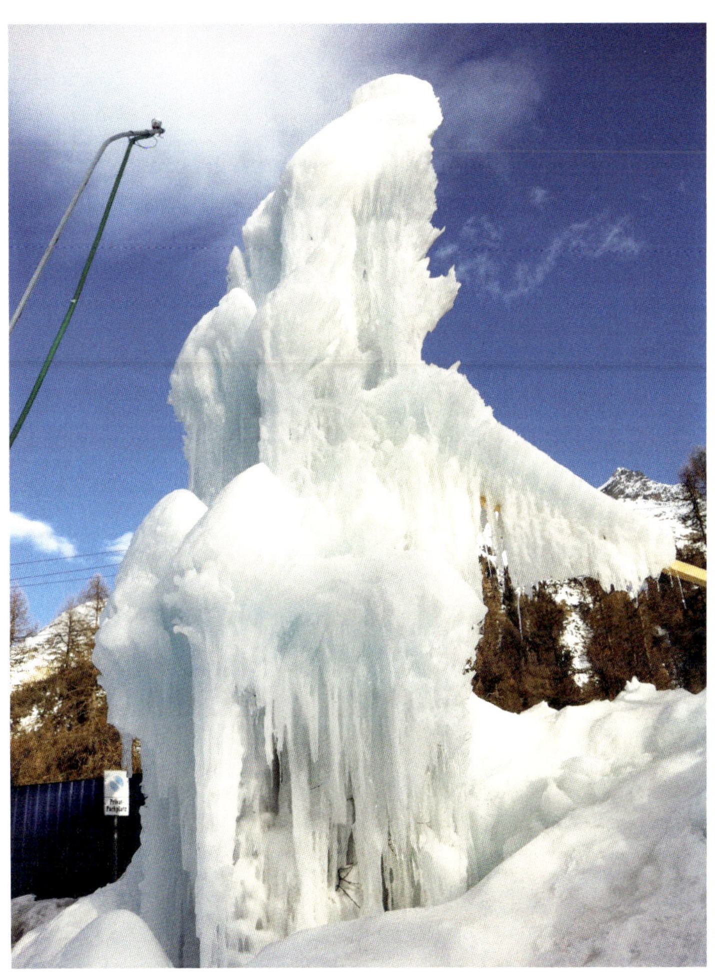

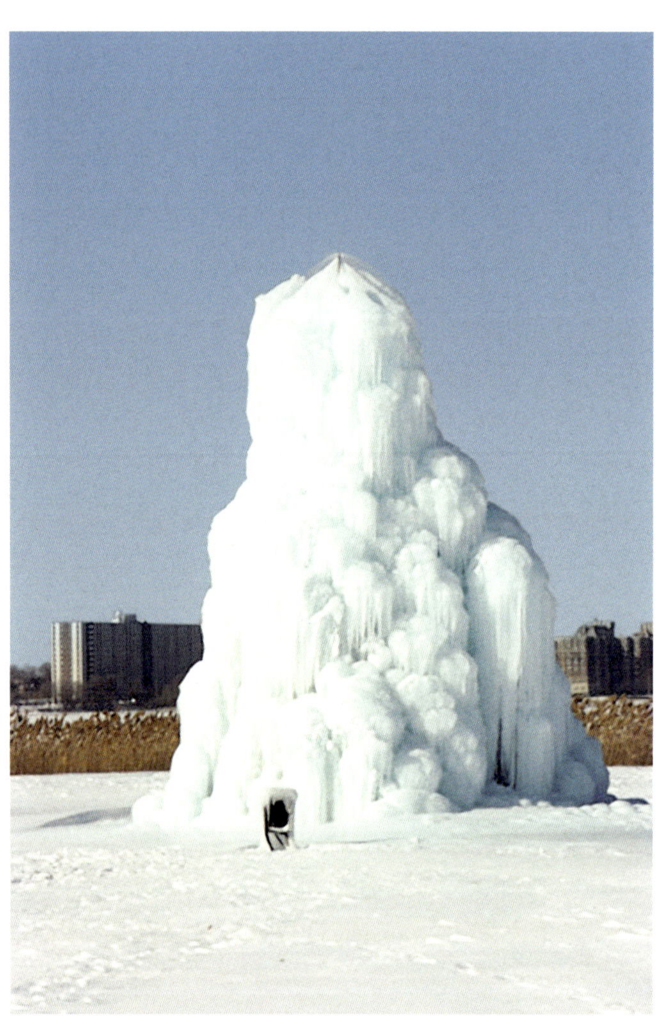

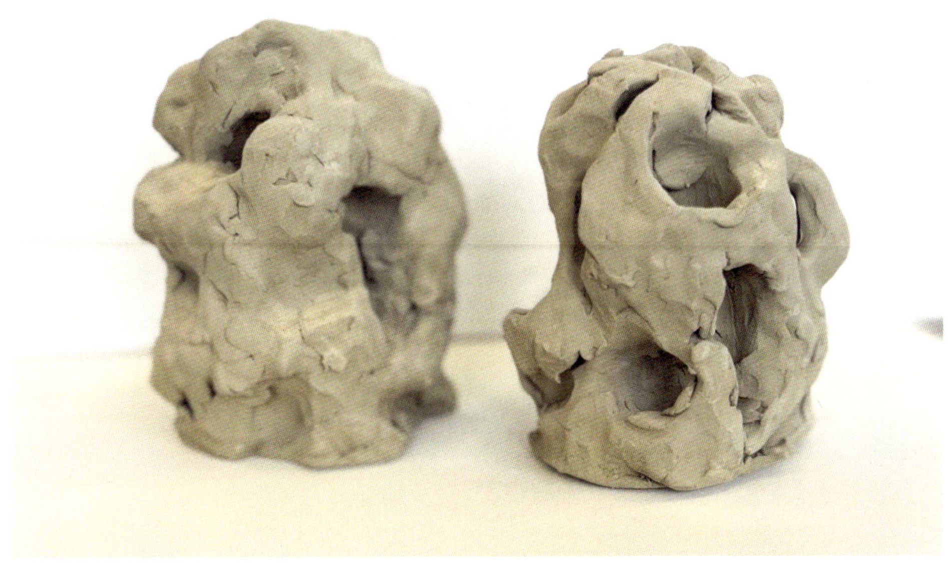

The popular opposites of *Gestalt* and *Ungestalt* are at play in a melting snowman, when form dissolves into anti-form in real time. A snowman in a freezer cannot disappear, despite efforts to the contrary. Yet, under these circumstances its facial expression and corpulence are unstable—its shape is constantly in flux, depending in on the atmospheric conditions and its internal temperature. Fischli/Weiss, *Zwei Ungestalten* from *Suddenly This Overview*, 1981–2012. Unfired clay

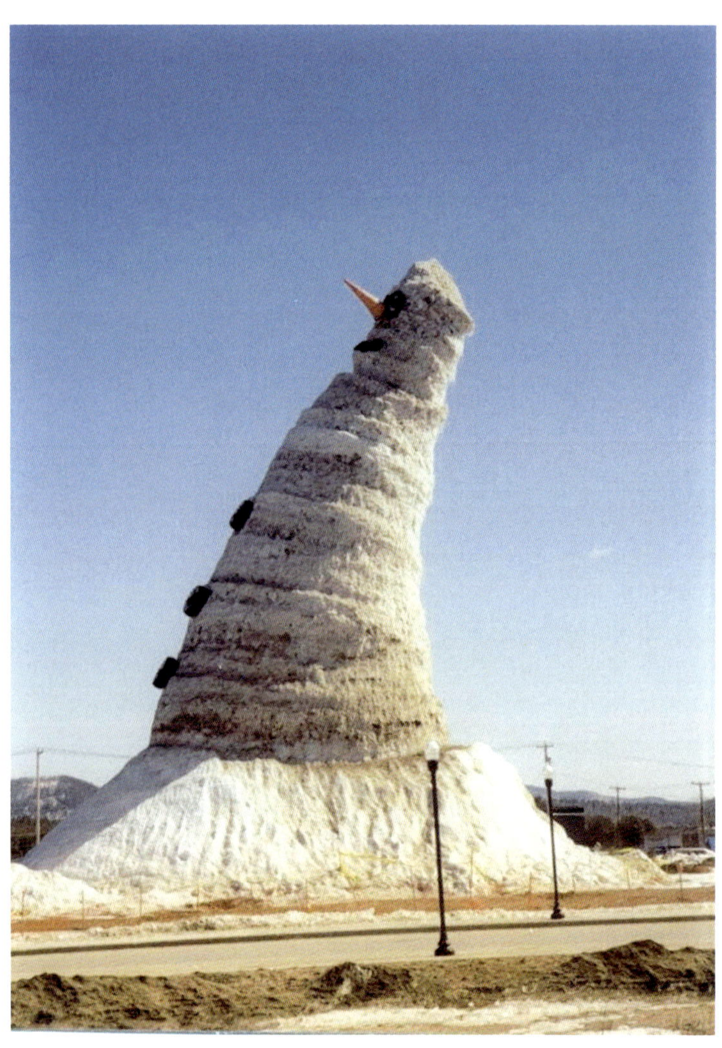

World's Tallest Snowman, Bethel, Maine, 1999. Height: 113 ft. 7 in. (10 stories); weight: 8,000,000 lbs.; diameter: 80 ft. Melted June 10, 1999. Titled "Angus, King of the Mountains" after Angus King, Maine's governor at the time, and US Senator since 2013

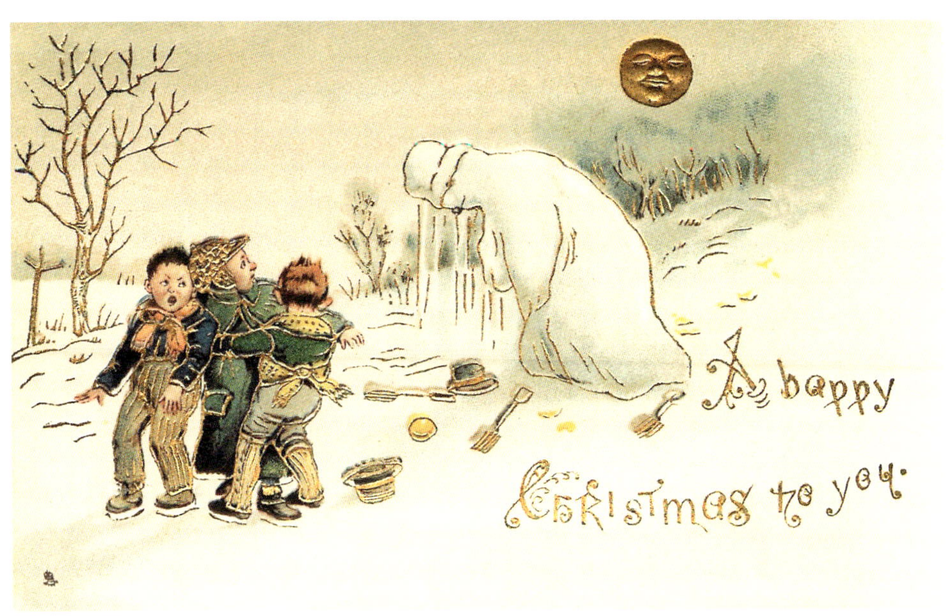

Christmas card depicting a melting snowman attacking children, ca. 1905

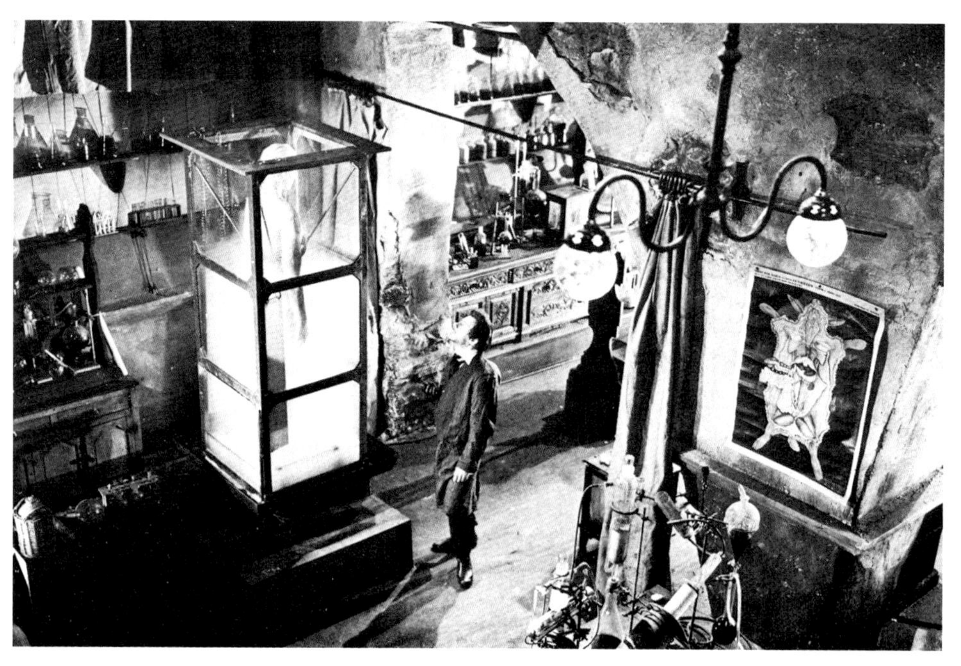

Film still from *The Revenge of Frankenstein*, 1958. Hammer/Columbia Pictures film

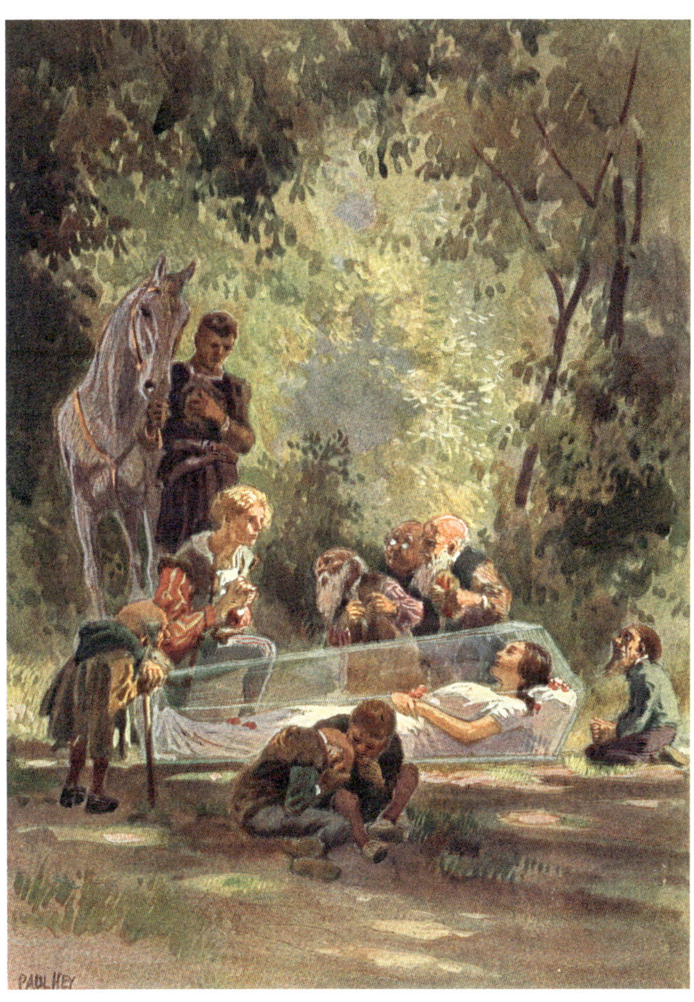

Frankenstein's monster and Snow White in their glass containers, in limbo. "Snow-White lay there in the coffin a long, long time," wrote Jacob and Wilhelm Grimm in 1812, "and she did not decay, but looked like she was asleep, for she was still as white as snow." *Snow White*. Postcard after a watercolor by Paul Hey (1867–1952) from the series "12 Fairytales"

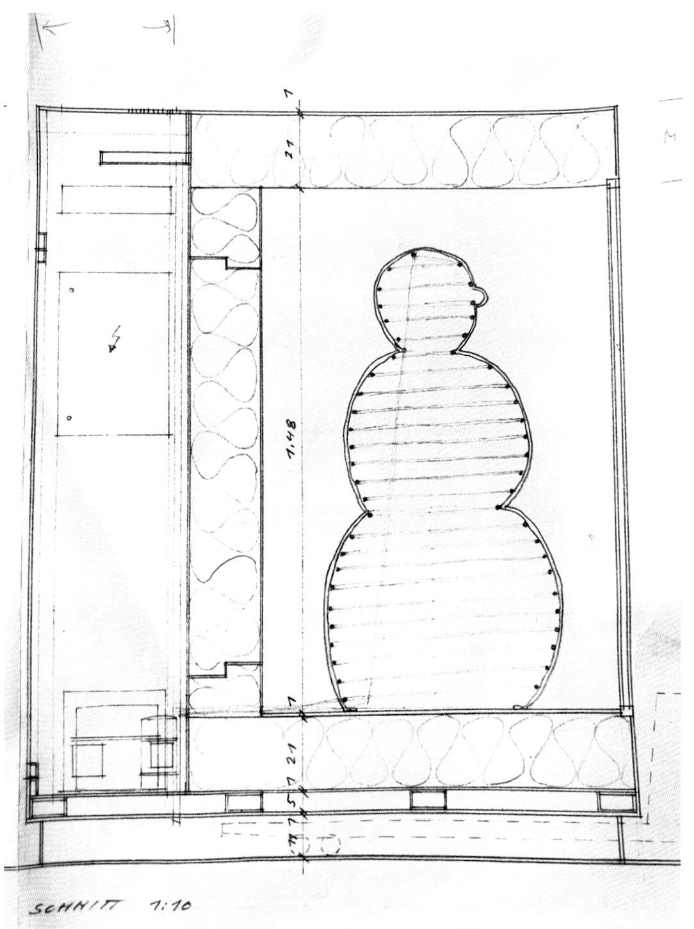

Nearly a decade after the unrealized Walker Art Center project, *Snowman* came to the United States, at the invitation of curator Susanne Ghez on behalf of the Art Institute of Chicago. Its design was partly revised and more concretely formulated based on notes and plans for the Walker project. Construction plan for revised variation of *Snowman*, 2016

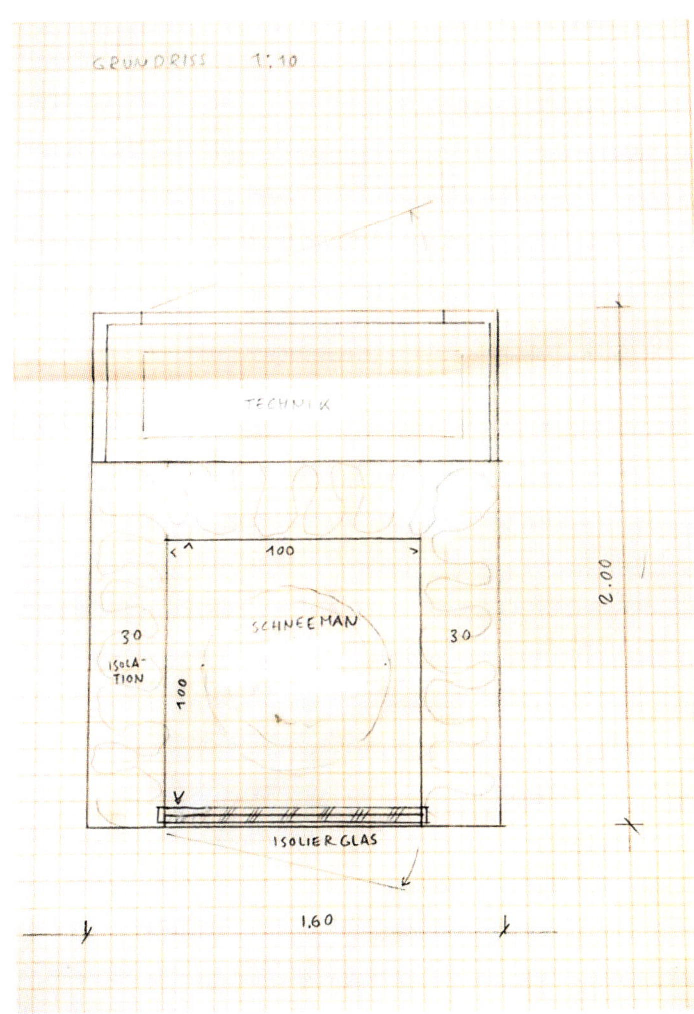
GRUNDRISS 1:10
TECHNIK
100
SCHNEEMAN
30
30
ISOLA-
TION
100
2.00
ISOLIERGLAS
1.60

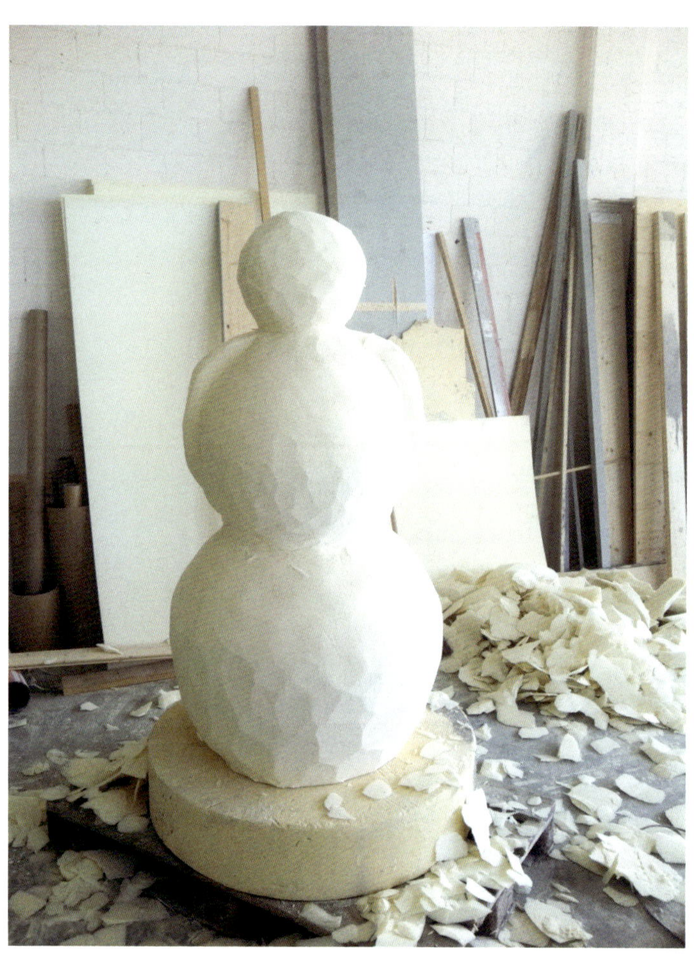

Model for revised *Snowman* in Fischli/Weiss studio, 2016. Polyurethane and wood

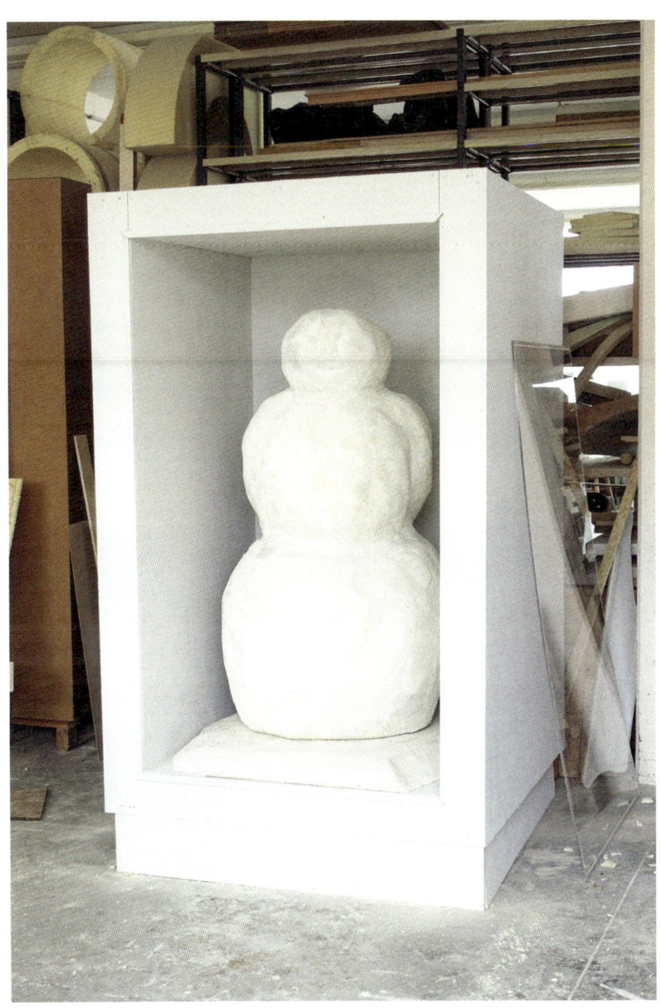

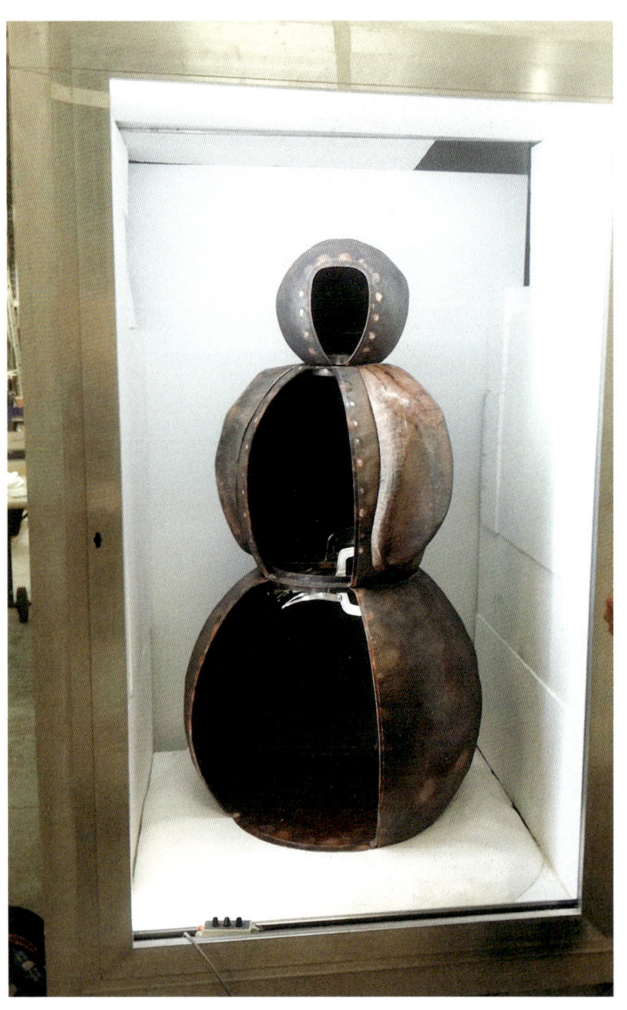

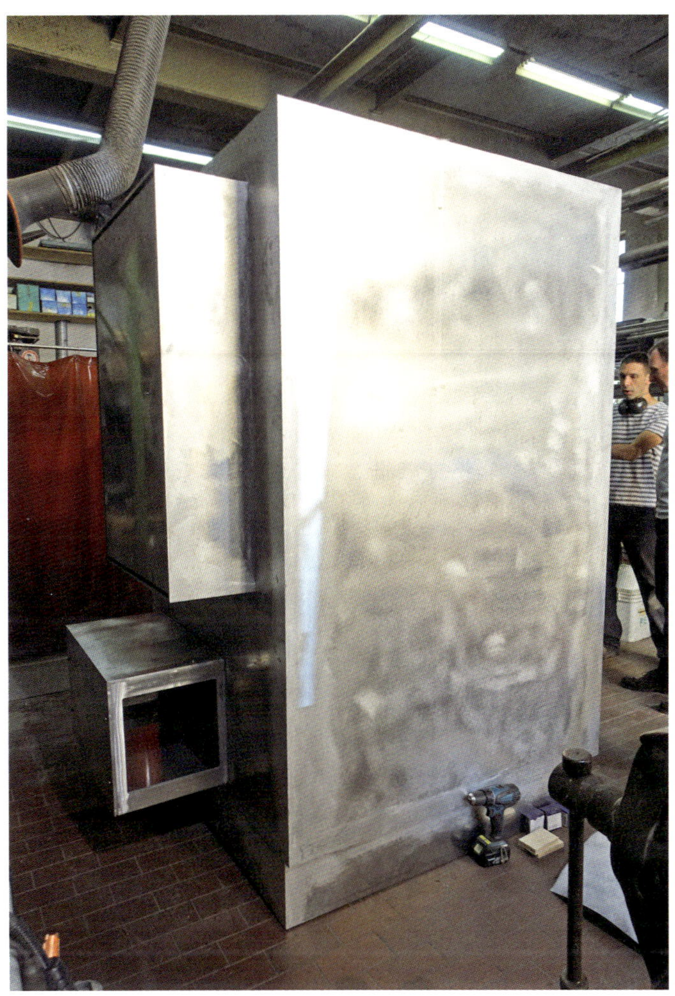

The refrigerator was executed in aluminum. The snowman skeleton was executed in tin-plated copper and outfitted with an interior cooling system—cooling pipes, thermostatic expansion valves, and a cooling unit—in order to regulate the temperature of the snow that builds up on its surface when the refrigerator is running. *Snowman* under construction and during technical tests at Kunstgiesserei St. Gallen, 2016

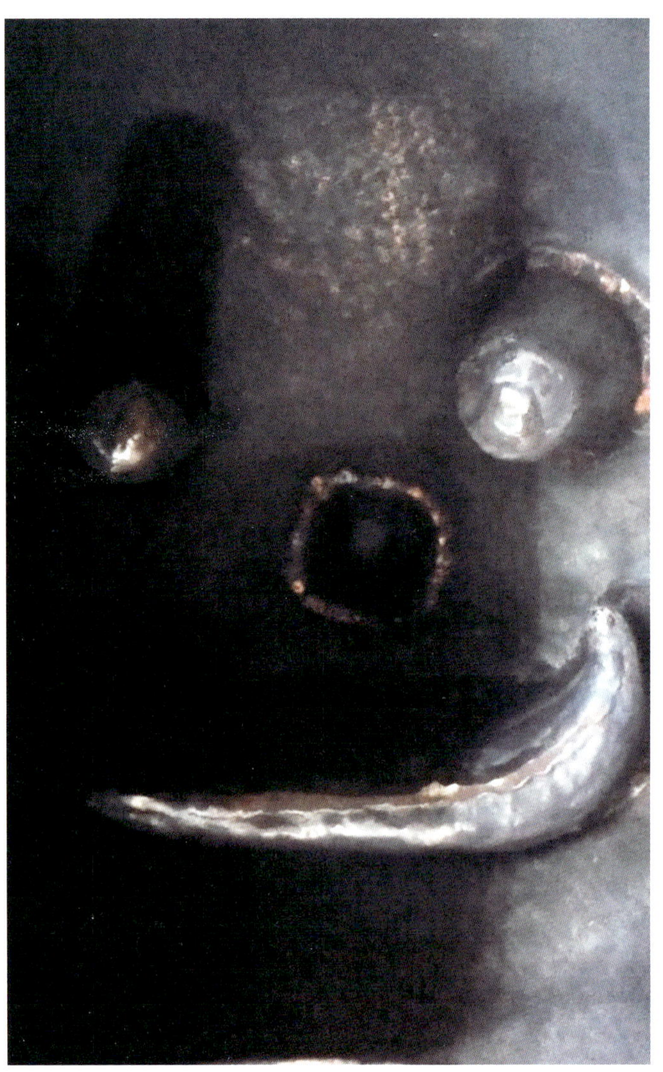

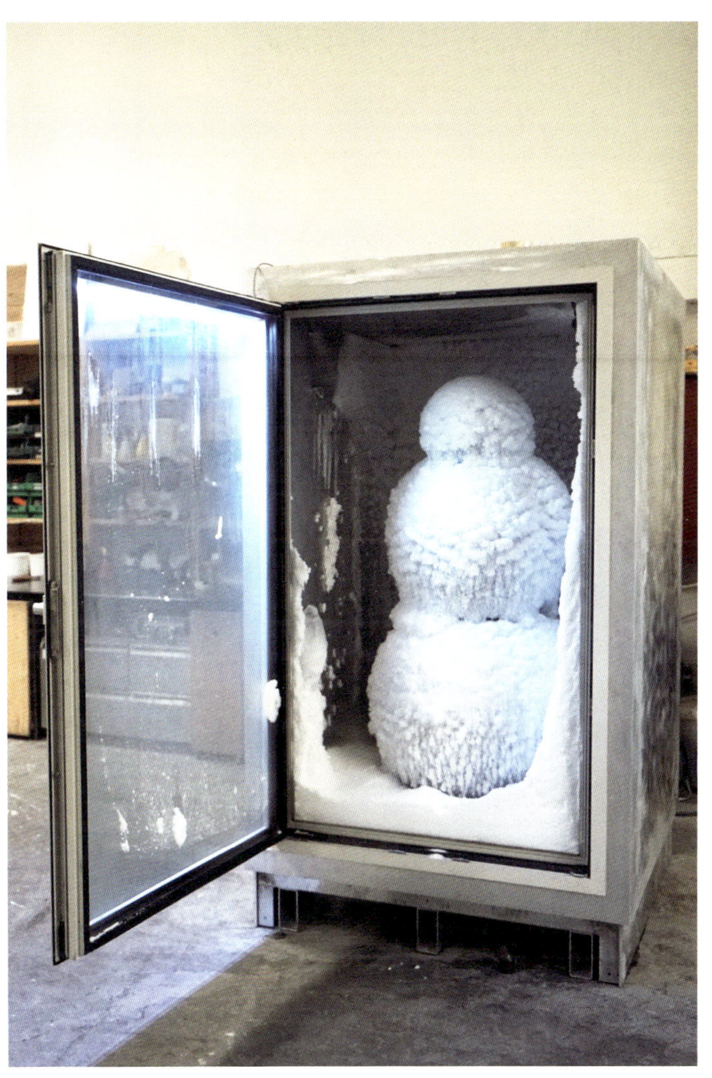

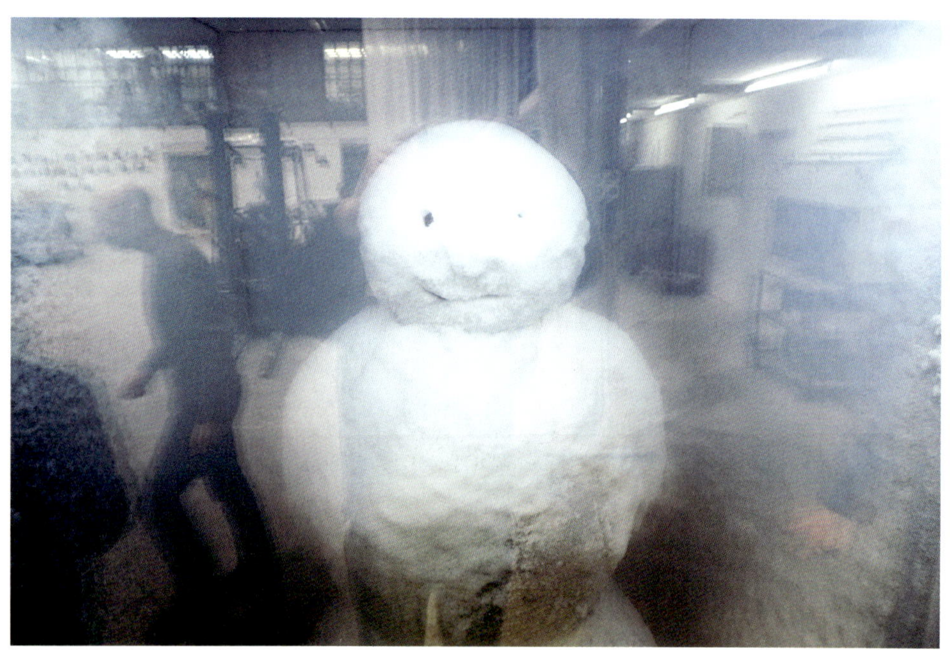

To ensure *Snowman's* sustainability throughout the summer, when temperatures rise, a provisory heated structure was built around the sculpture and a heat lamp was pointed in front of the glass vitrine. Changes in the expression of its face under these conditions were observed and adjustments were made.

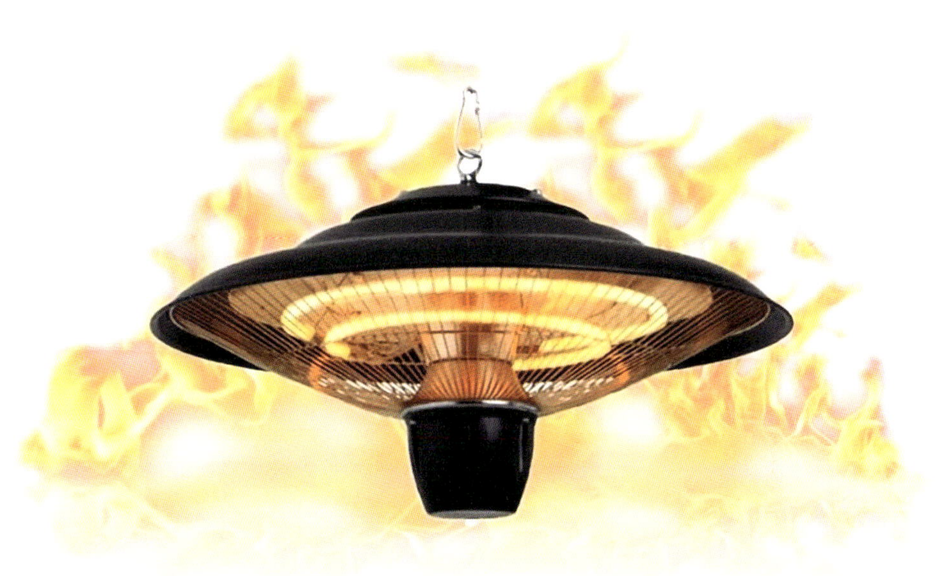

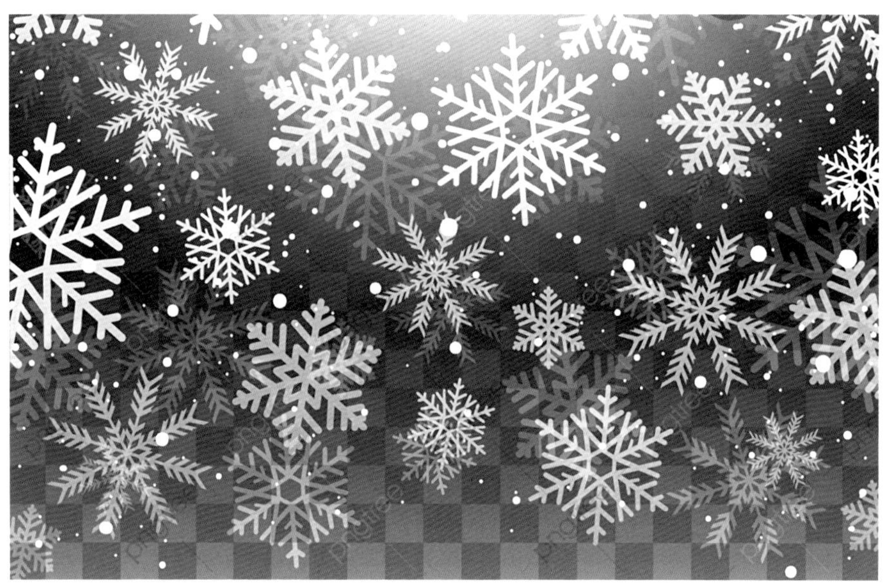

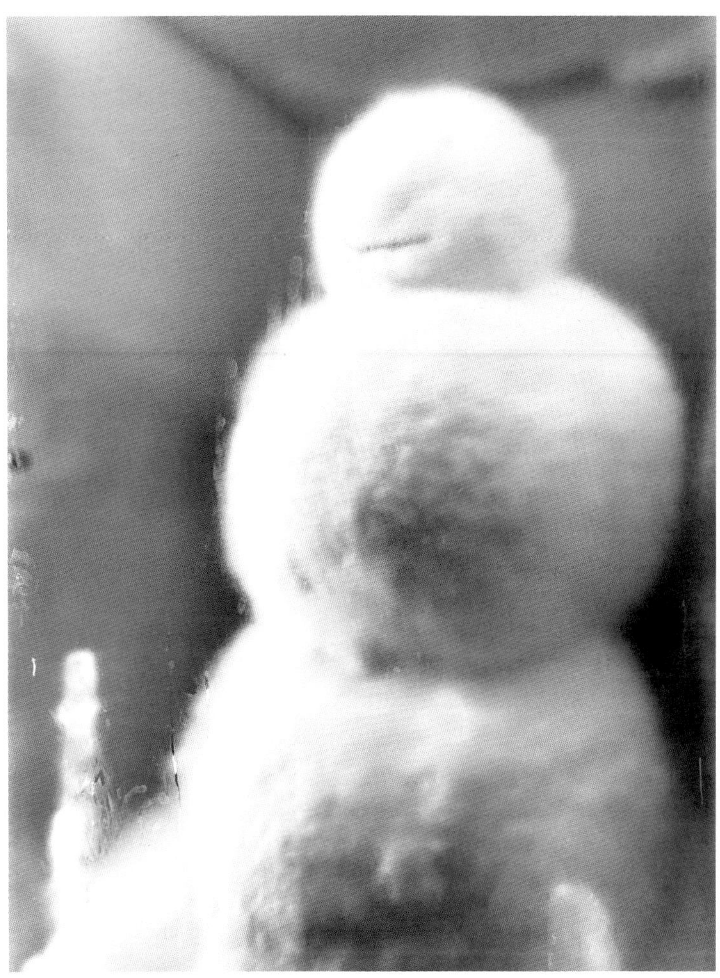

In order to build up the snow, water vapor was emitted inside the vitrine every hour for approximately five minutes at a time. During this process, the snowman's form became temporarily blurred and nearly invisible by the mist.

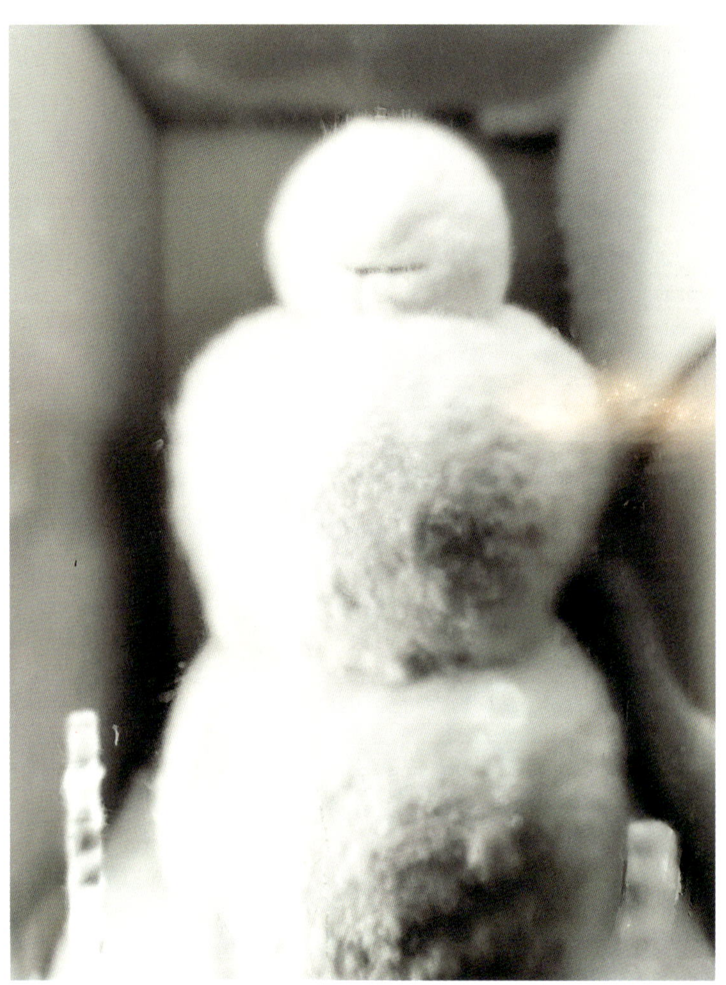

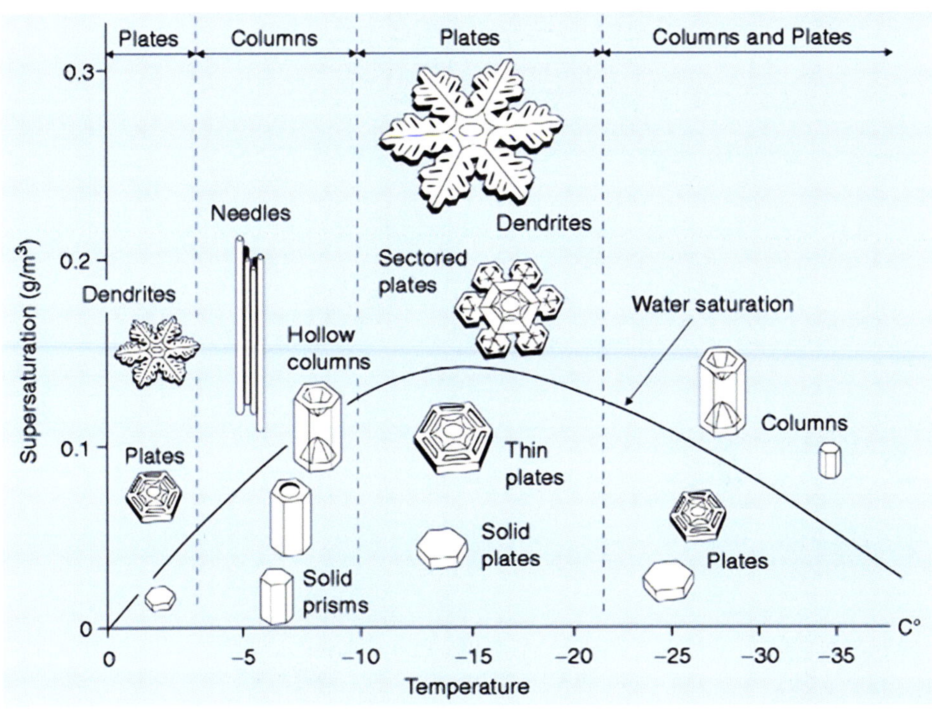

Diagram of snowflake typologies

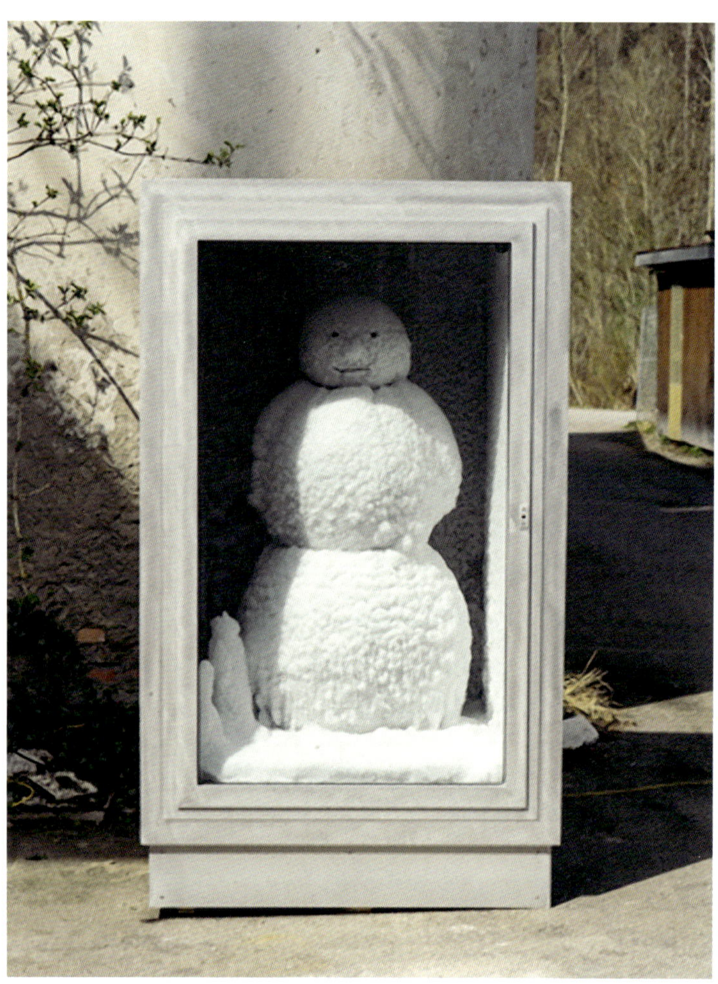

After its construction was complete, *Snowman* was installed and powered up outside the fabricator's building for several weeks in order to test its viability in the elements. Fischli / Weiss, *Snowman*, 1987/2016. Copper, aluminum, glass, water, and coolant system. 218 × 128 × 165 cm

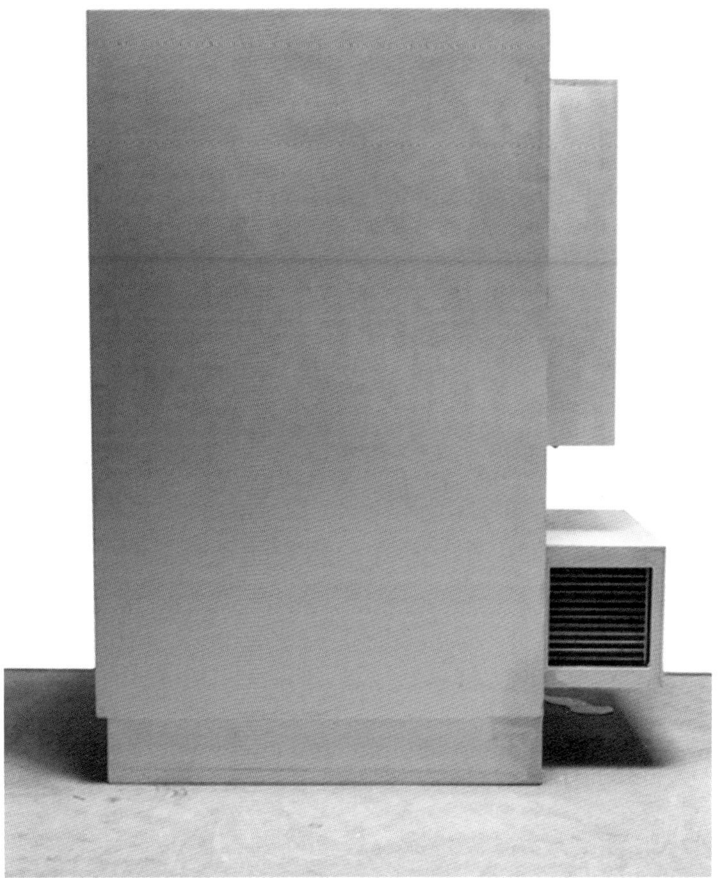

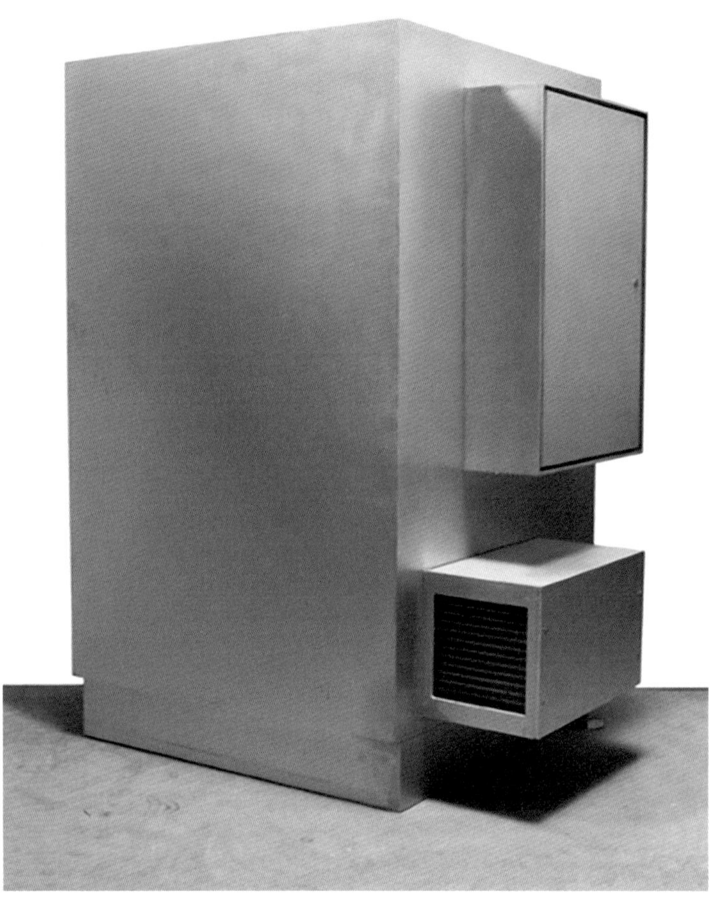

The technical equipment was integrated into two very pronounced rectangular compartments at the back of the unit: the upper compartment houses the control gauges for temperature, pressure, and humidity, and the lower compartment houses the cooling system, including the compressor, condenser, evaporator, and expansion valve.

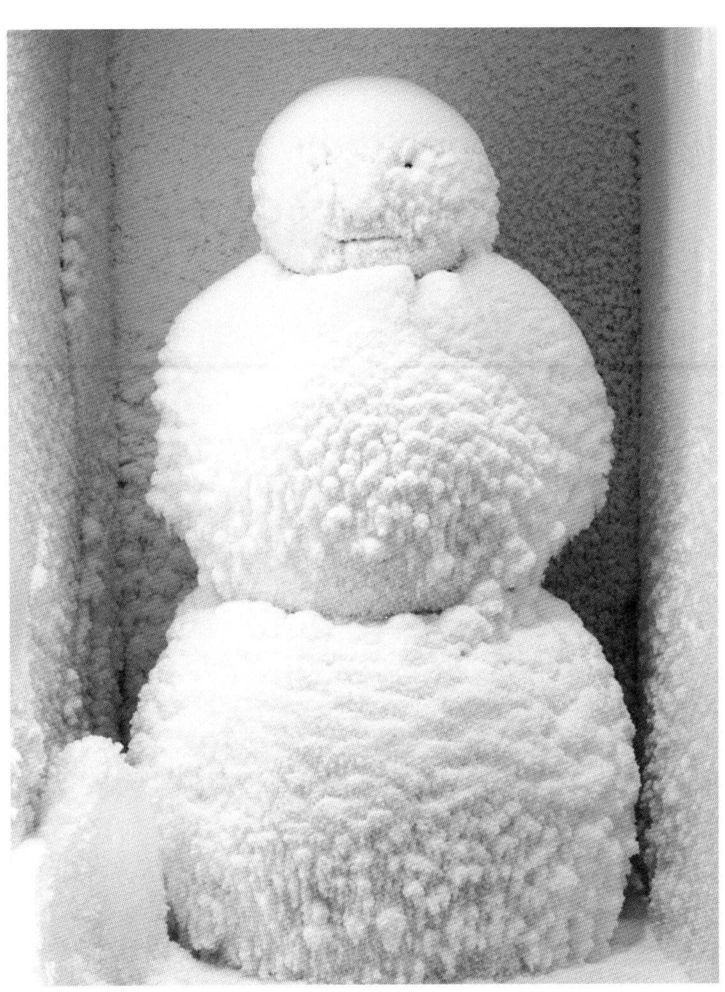

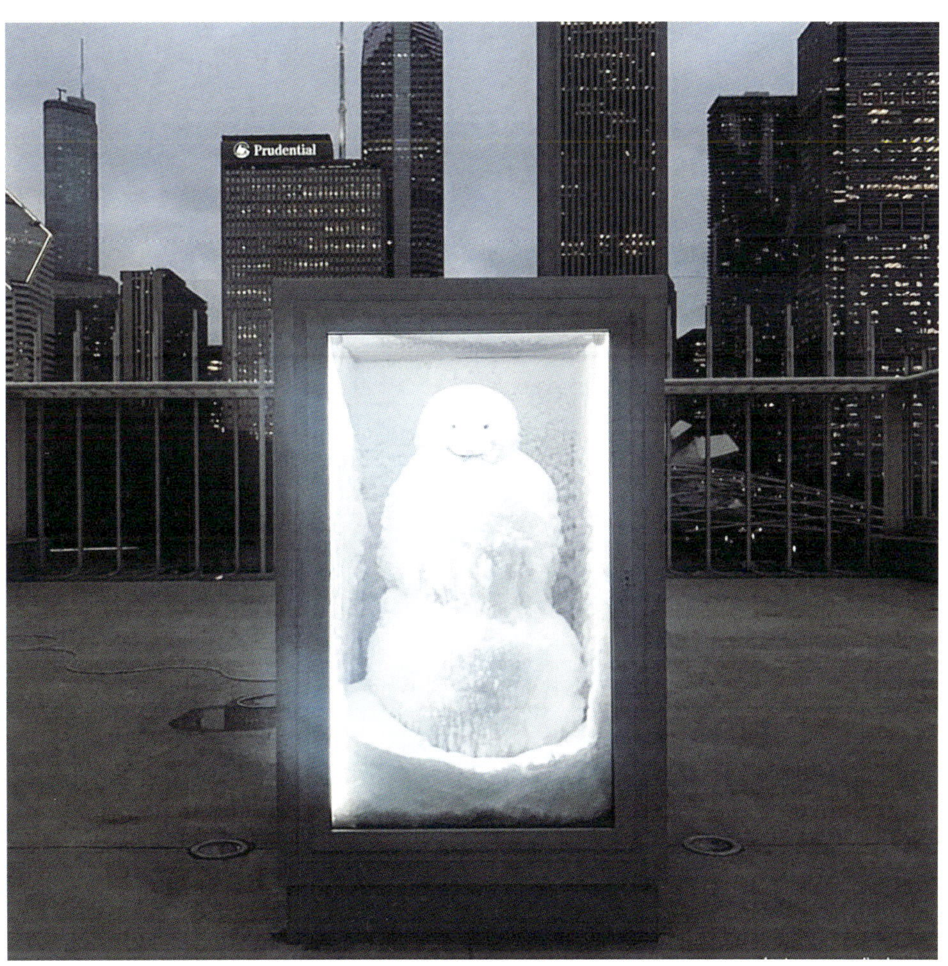
Prudential

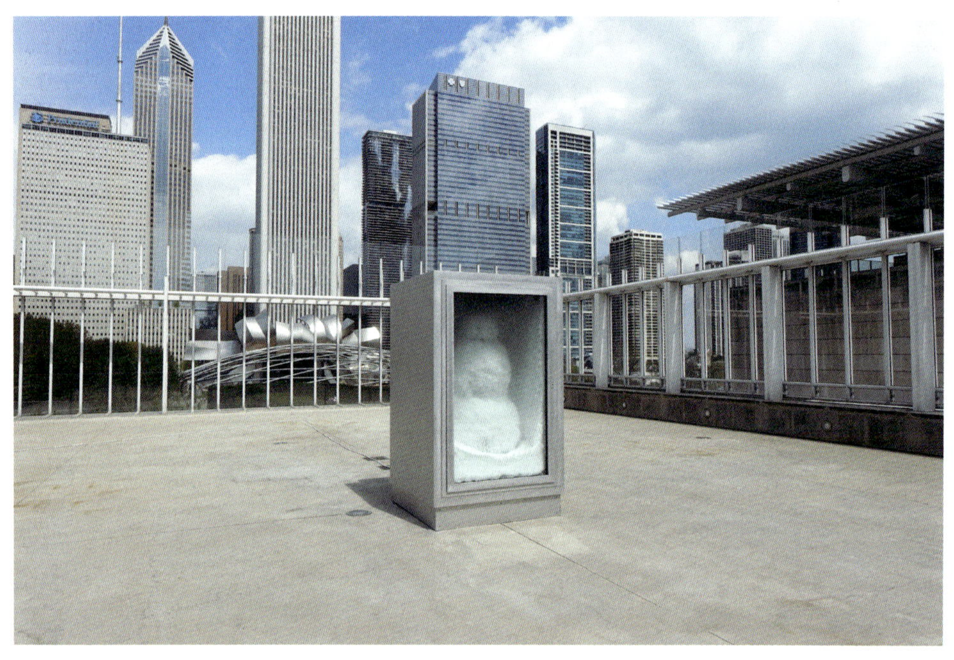

Snowman installed on the terrace at the Art Institute of Chicago, April 27–October 15, 2017. Organized by Susanne Ghez. Here, the sculpture was presented alone—a solitaire in an urban landscape. During the summer months, temperatures on the shadowless terrace can reach 100°F or higher. In fact, on July 14, 1954, it was reportedly 117°F. On August 4, 2017, the hottest day in Chicago that summer, the temperature on the terrace was recorded at 96°F. *Snowman* made it through this heatwave, though its appearance changed slightly—its facial features sagged a bit under the humid snow, and some sensitive viewers expressed compassion.

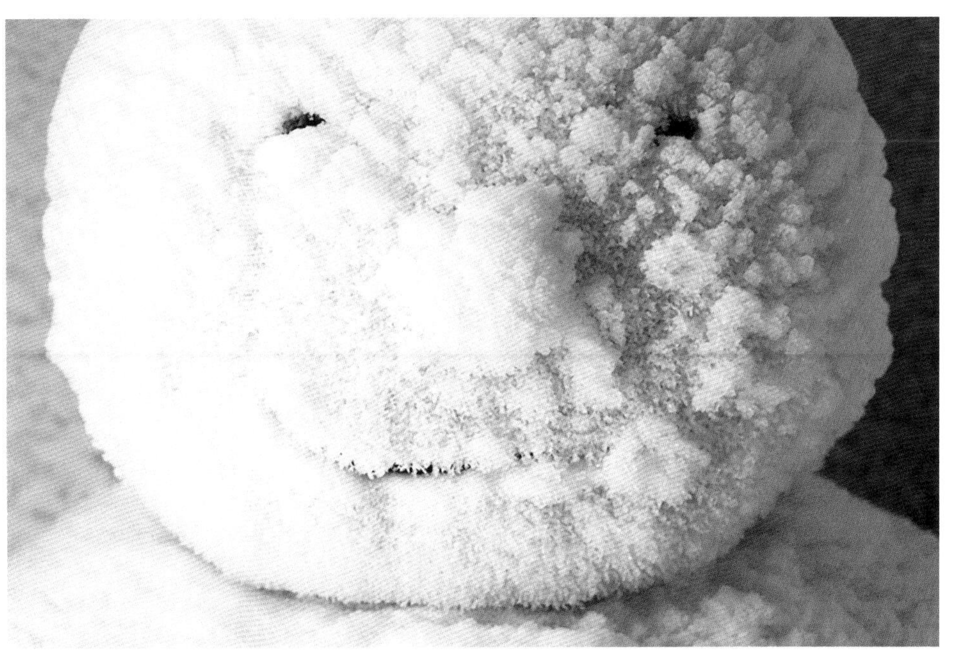

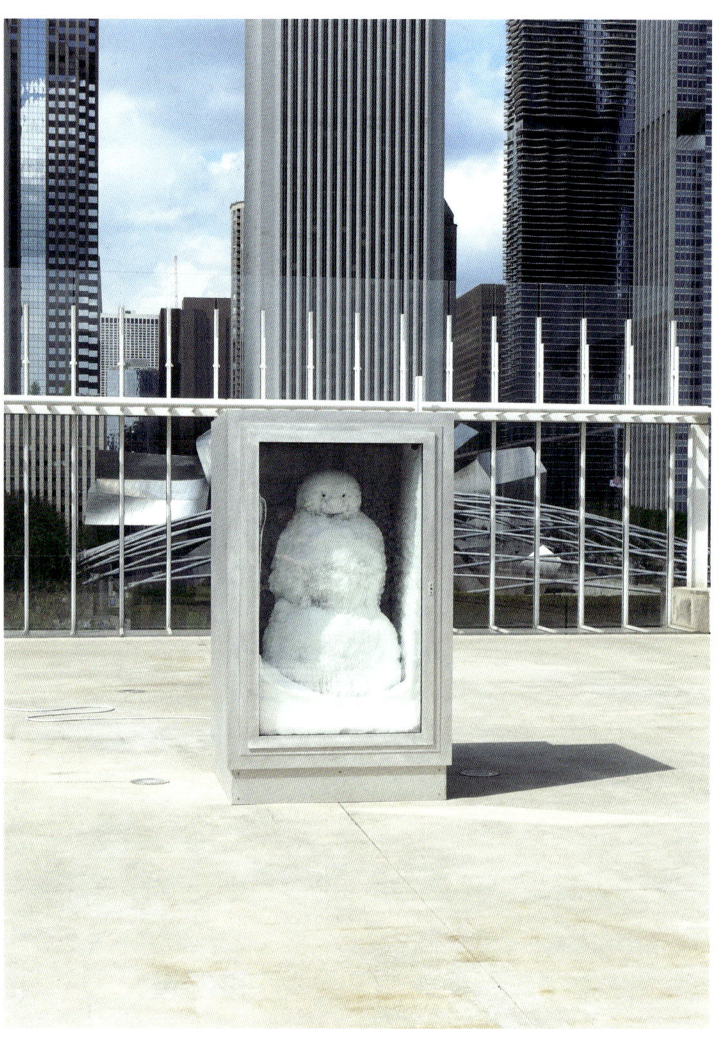

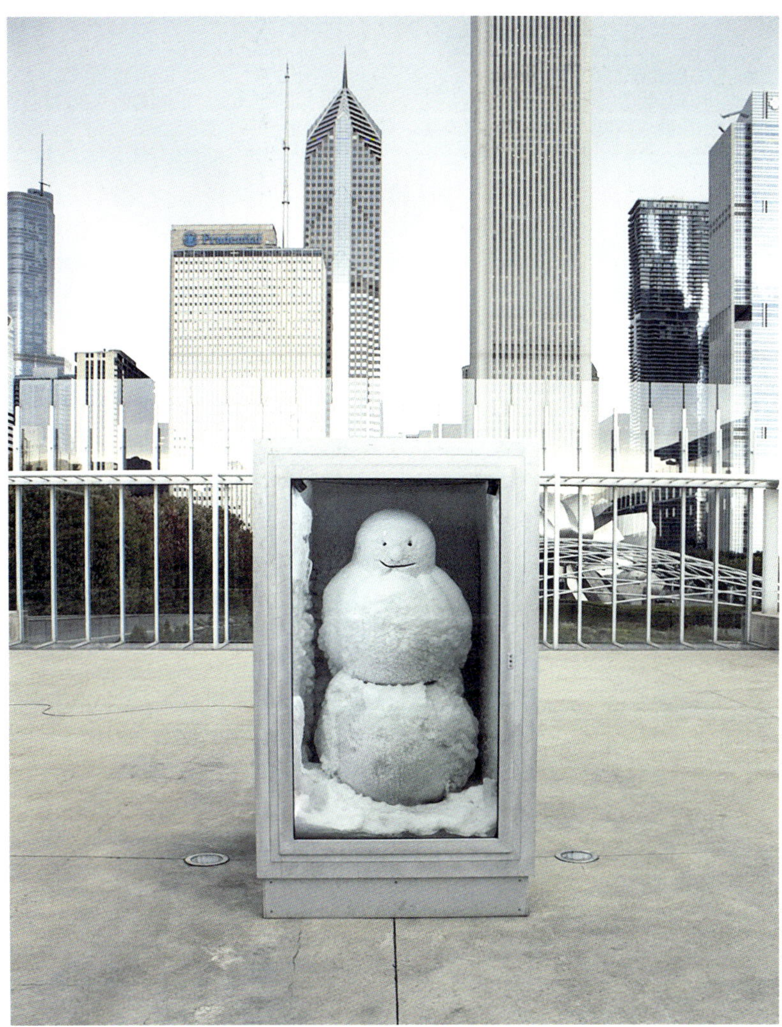
Prudential

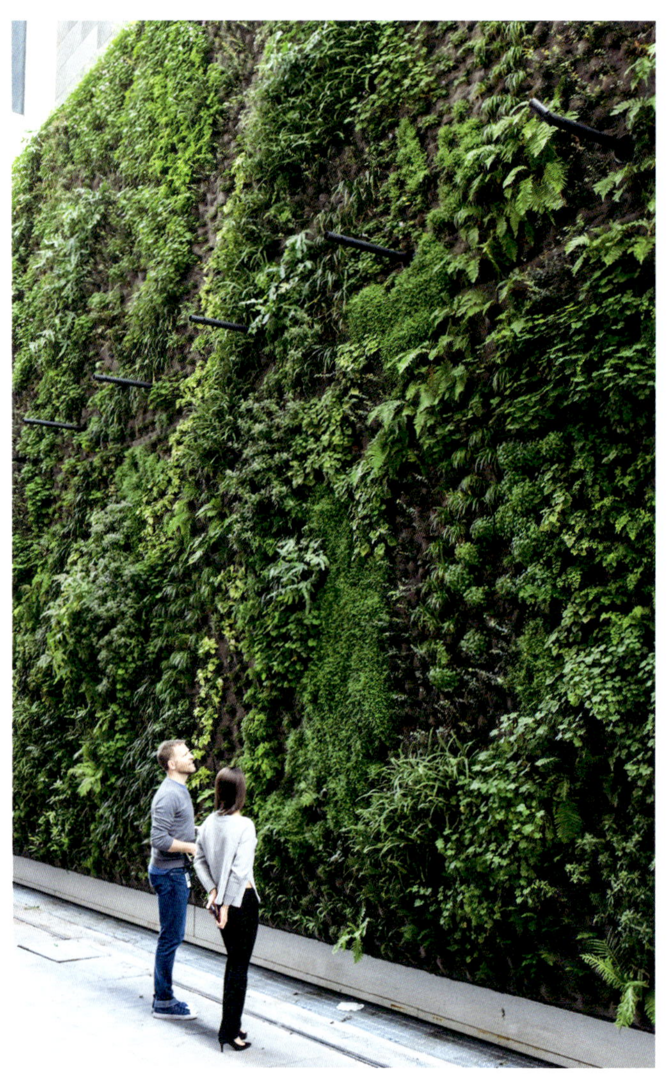

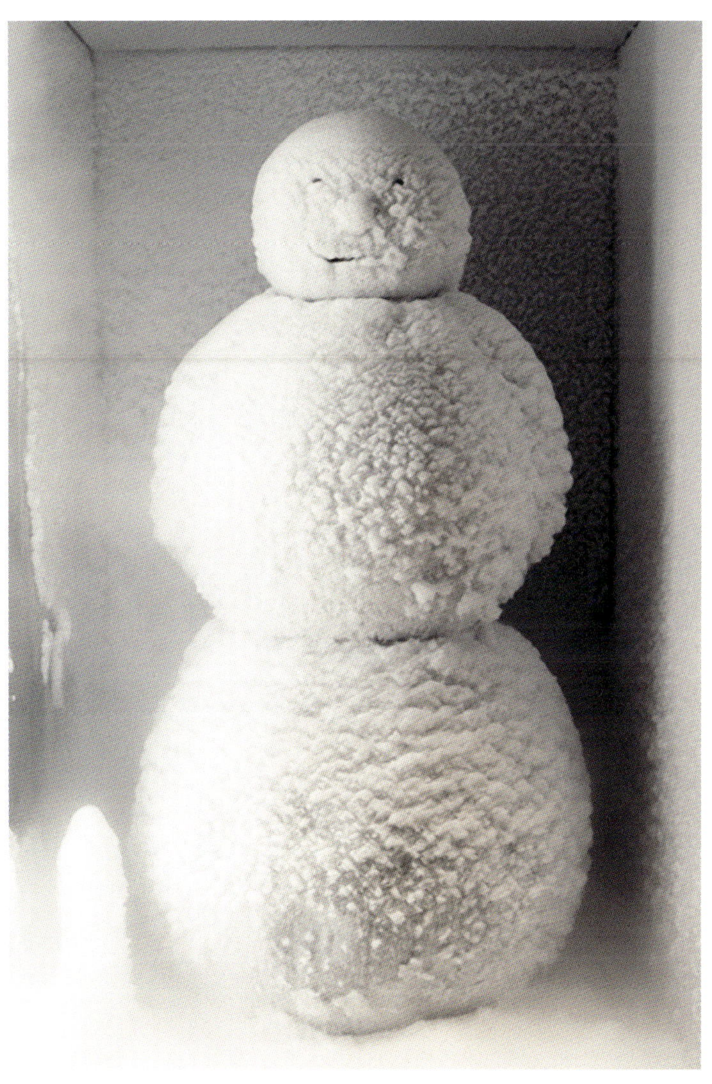

Snowman installed on the sculpture terrace at SFMOMA, December 2, 2017–May 23, 2018. Organized by Gary Garrels

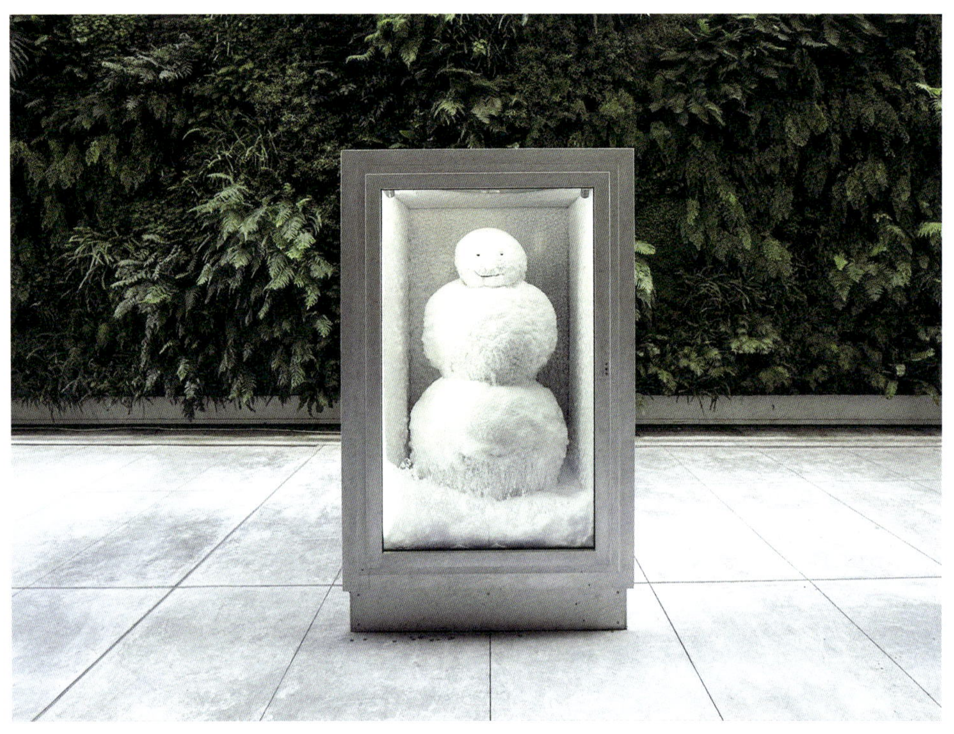

Here, the sculpture was presented in front of a “living wall” designed by Habitat Horticulture, featuring 19,442 plants of 37 species.

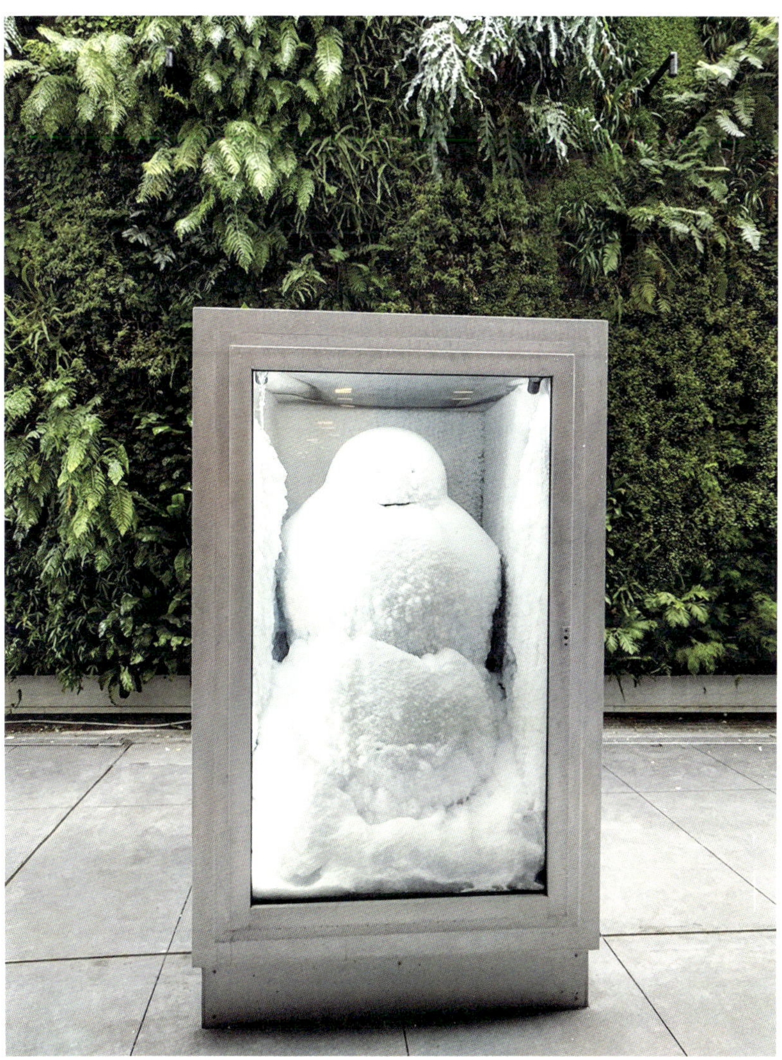

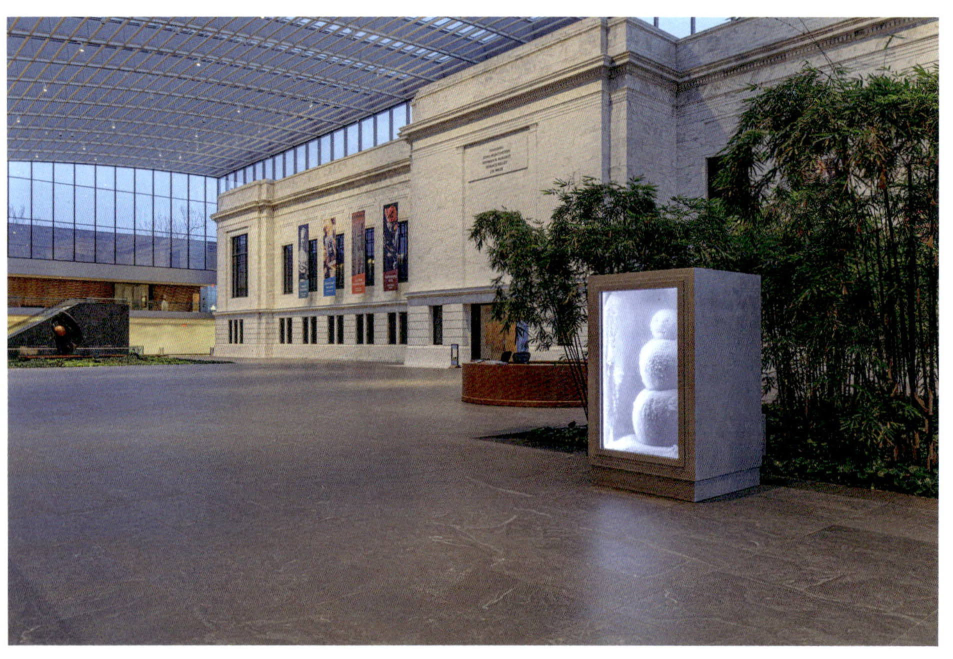

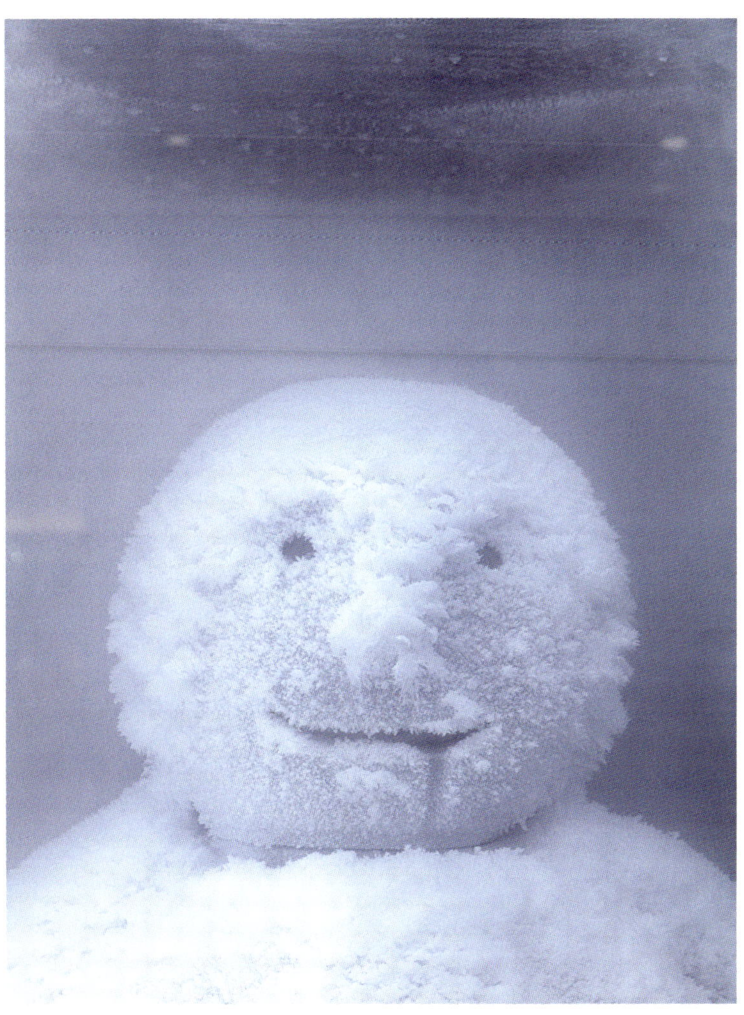

Two years after its presentation at SFMOMA, *Snowman* had a second encounter with composed greenery, this time in an interior atrium space—in front of a building within a building. *Snowman* installed at the Cleveland Museum of Art, January 7–September 6, 2020. Organized by Emily Liebert

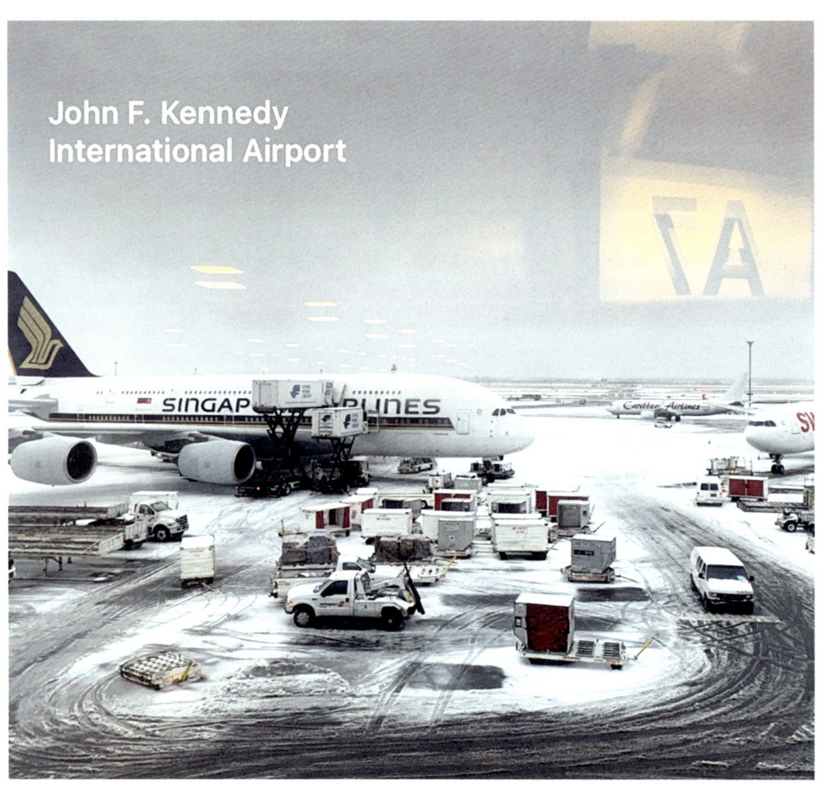

In February 2018, a meeting was arranged at MoMA to determine a possible site for *Snowman* to be presented there the following summer.

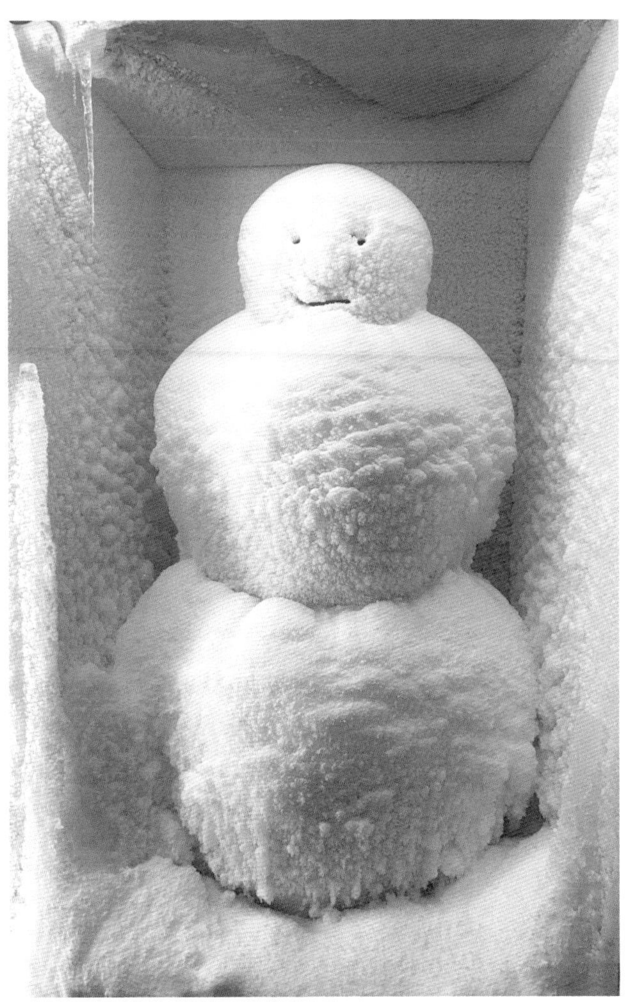

Snowman installed in the exhibition *If Everything Is Sculpture, Why Make Sculpture?* in the Abby Aldrich Rockefeller Sculpture Garden at The Museum of Modern Art, June 12, 2018–May 10, 2019. Organized by Peter Fischli and Cara Manes. Here, *Snowman* was presented alongside twenty-three works, largely from MoMA's collection, who became its new neighbors for the duration of the exhibition.

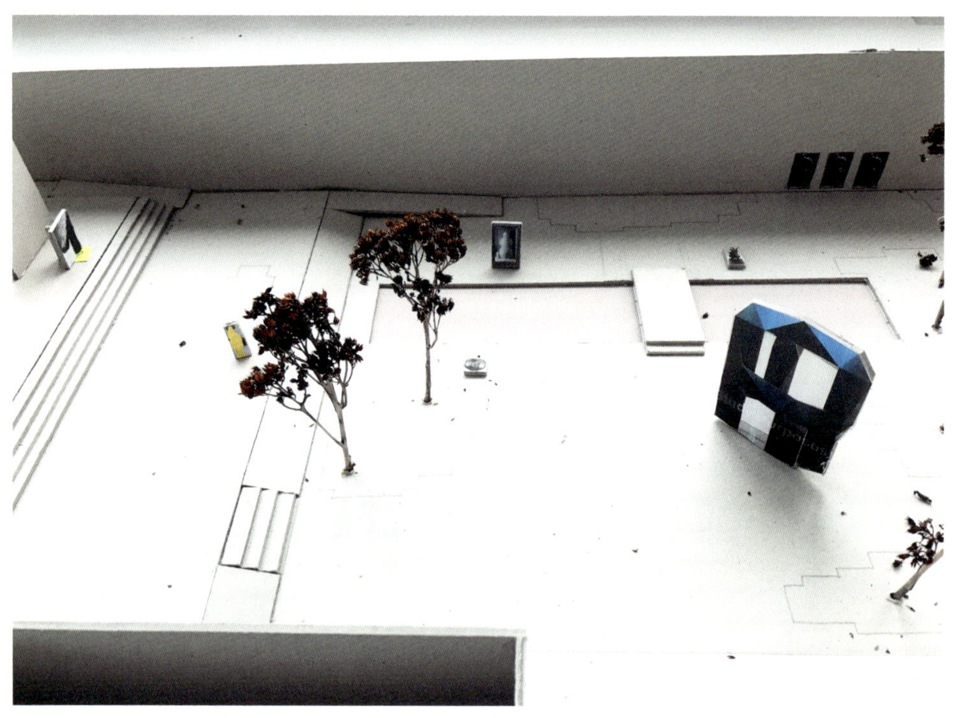

Cardboard model for MoMA exhibition in the studio, April 2018

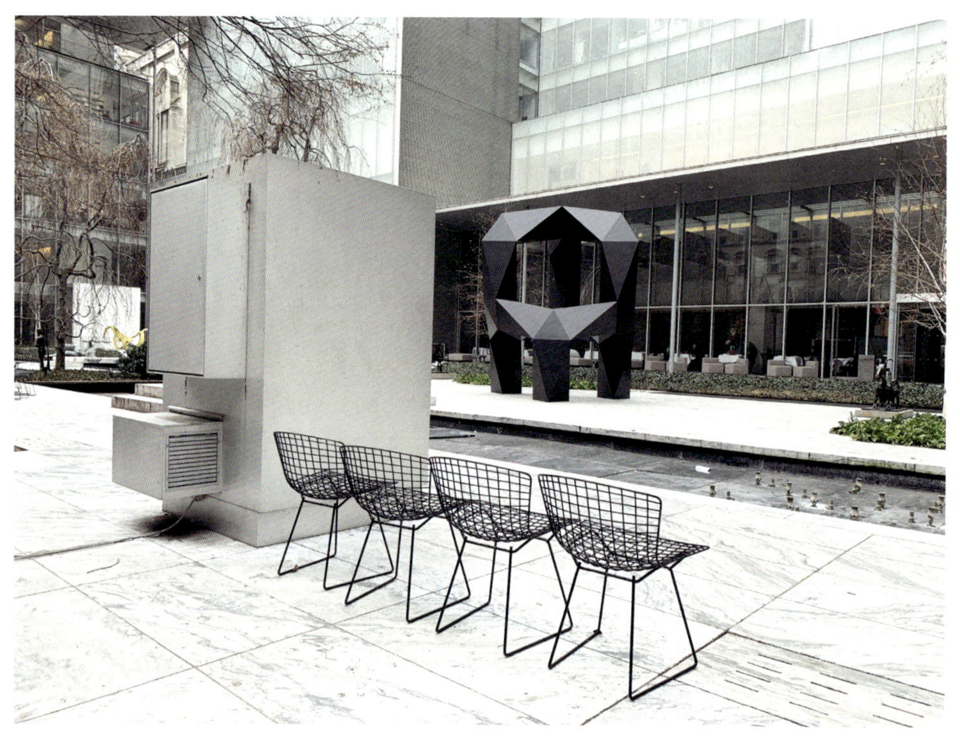

Snowman with Tony Smith, *Moondog,* 1964 (fabricated 1998). Painted aluminum

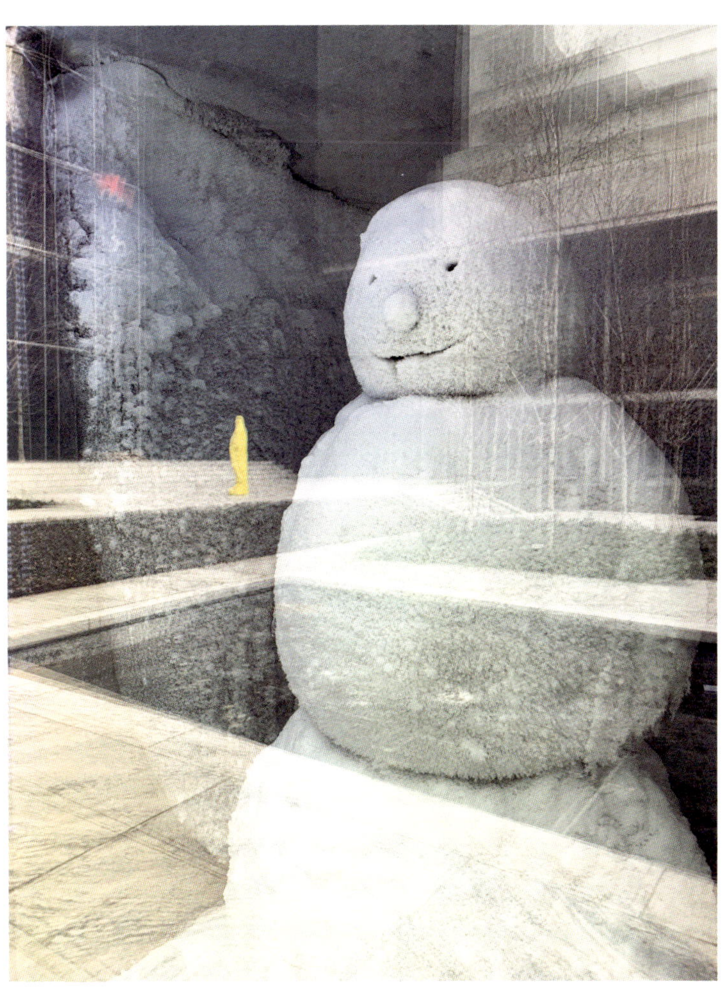

Snowman with reflection of Katharina Fritsch, *Yellow Madonna* from *Group of Figures*, 2006–08 (fabricated 2010–11). Copper, lacquered

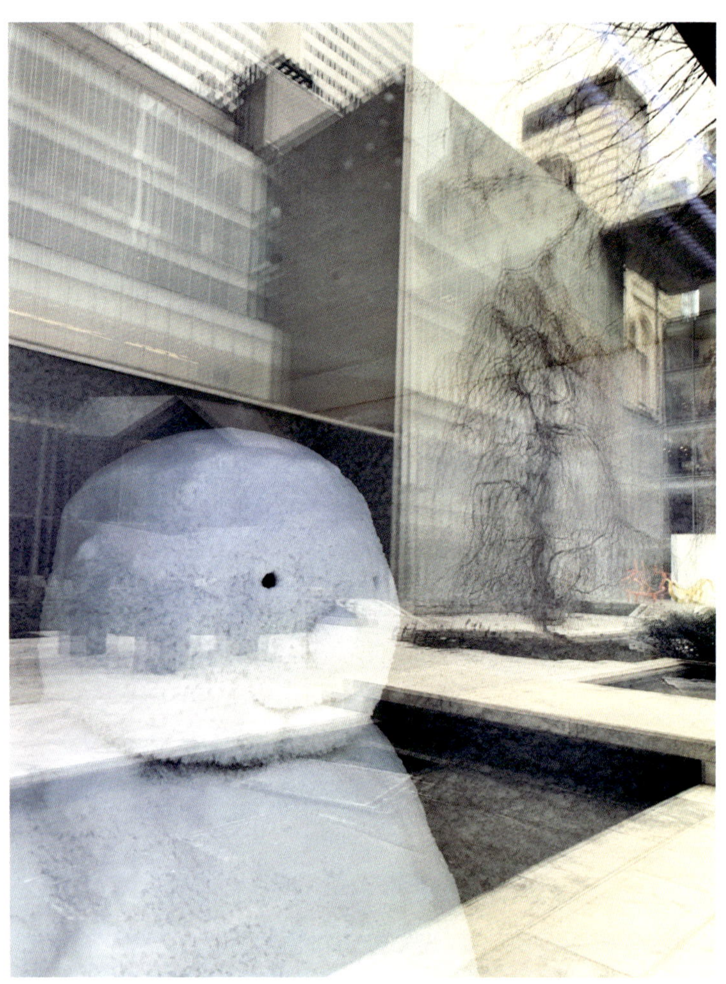

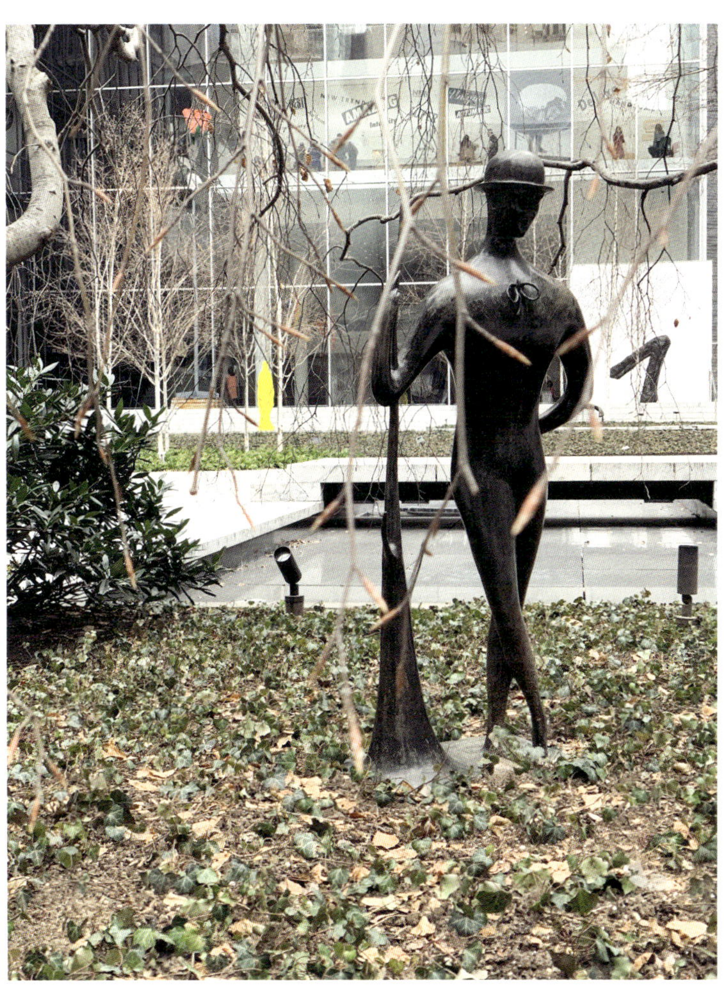

Snowman with Elie Nadelman, *Man in the Open Air*, ca. 1915. Bronze

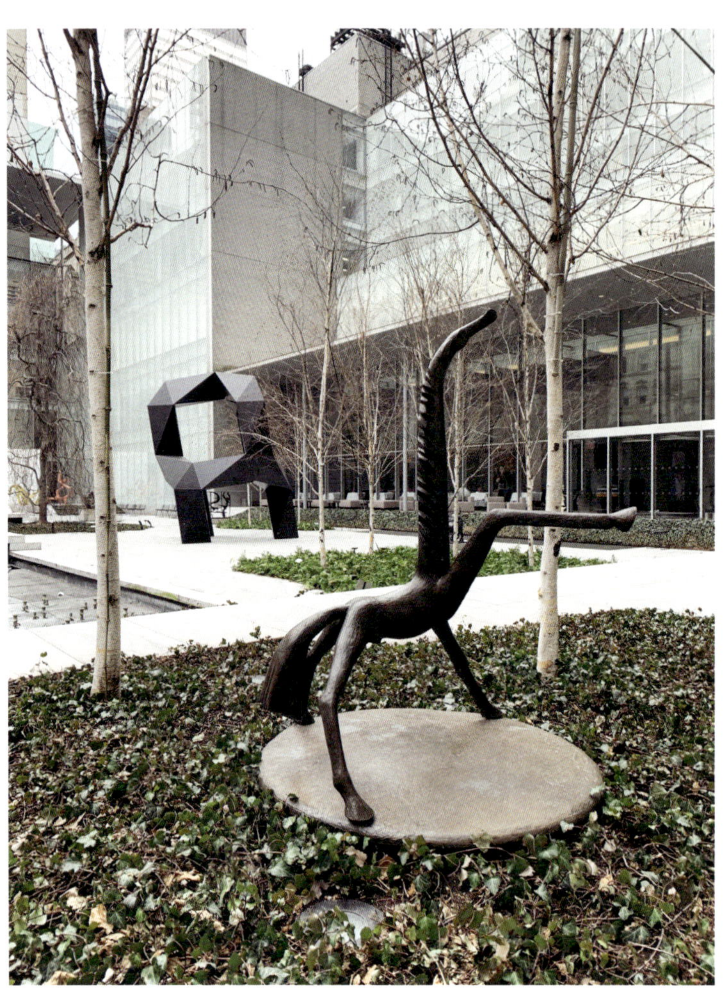

Snowman with Mary Callery, *Horse*, 1942. Bronze

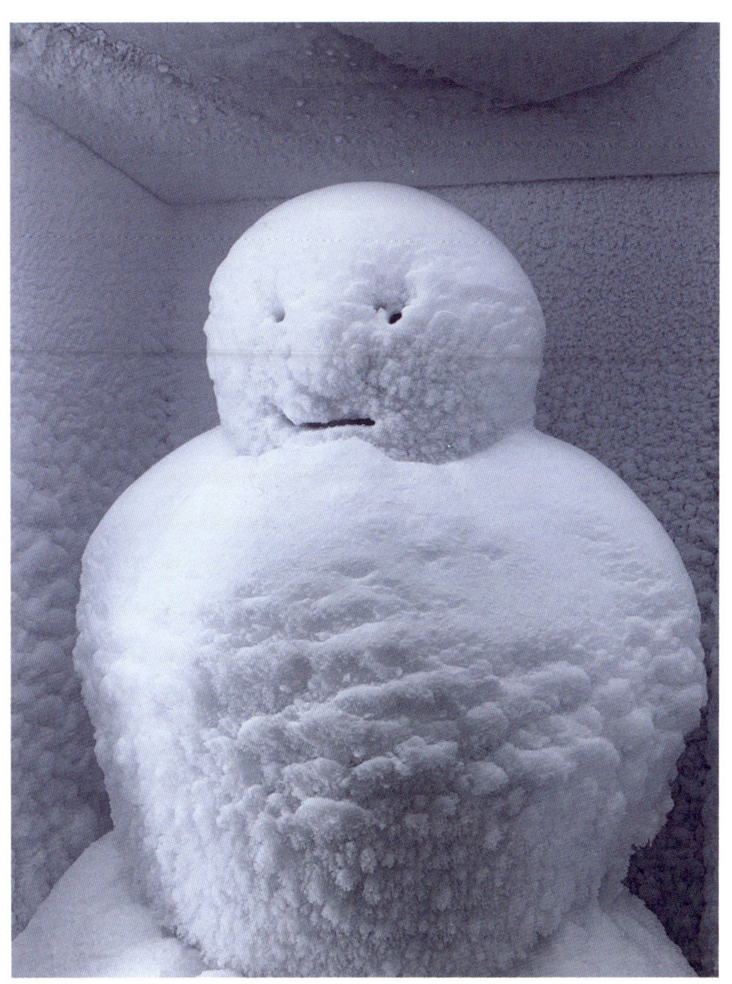

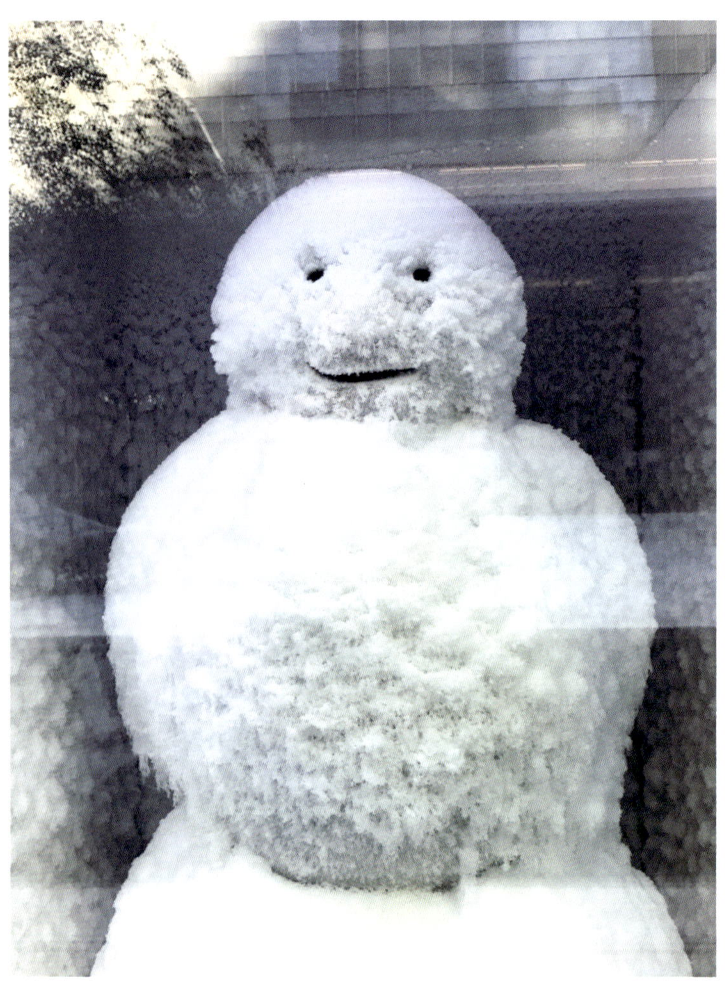

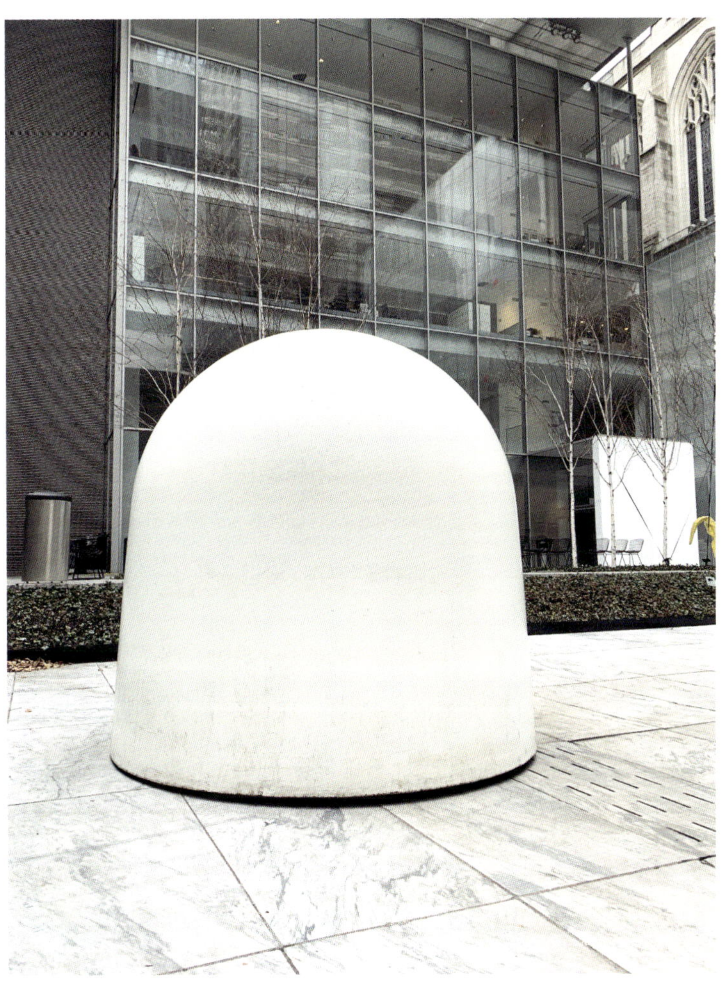

Snowman with Robert Breer, *Osaka I*, 1970. Self-propelled sculpture with fiberglass shell, steel frame, battery-driven motor, and rubber-tire wheels

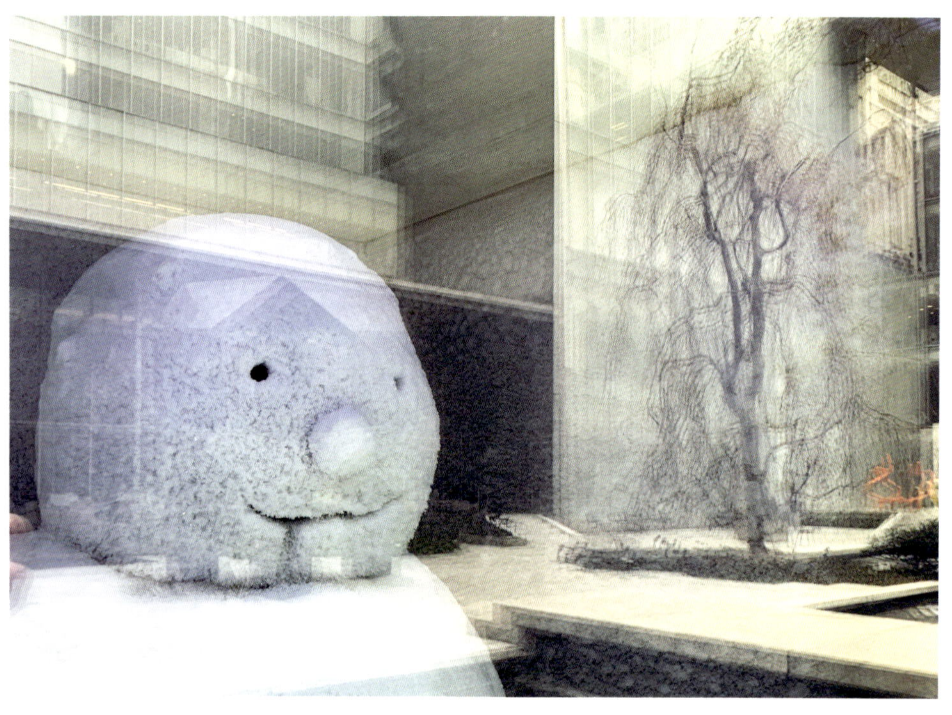

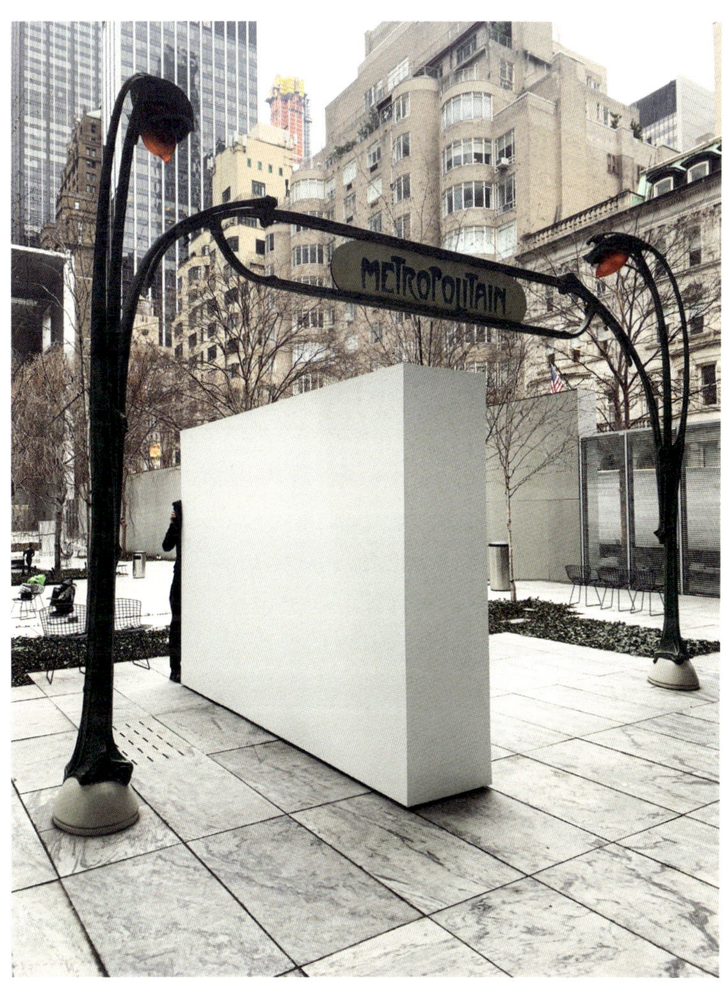

Snowman with Peter Fischli and Wade Guyton, *Untitled Aspen Wall Nr. 6*, 2016 and 2018. Rubber, steel plate, anchors, metal framing, screws, fiberglass mat sheathing, corner bead, exterior joint compound, liquid vapor barrier, elastometric paint

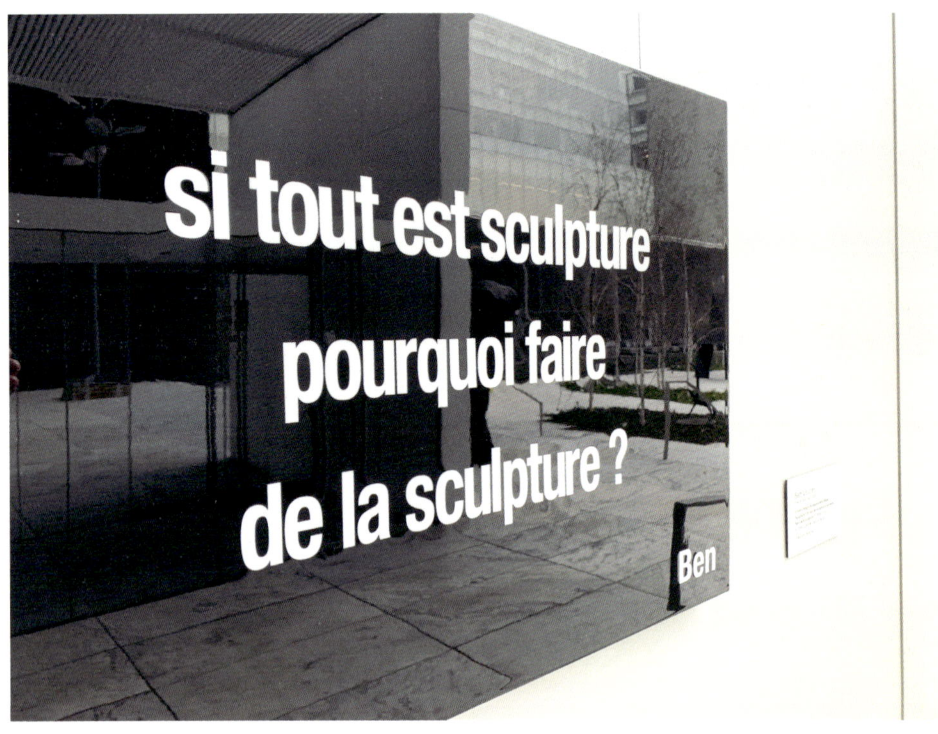

This exhibition featured a painting displayed in the MoMA garden—a painting that Ben Vautier first made for an outdoor sculpture exhibition in 1995. Its subject provided the title of the show in the museum's "Artist's Choice" series: *If Everything Is Sculpture, Why Make Sculpture?* A snowman is a sculpture that almost anyone can make by rolling and stacking three balls of snow. In this sense, there is an inherent absence of artistic creativity in developing the form; its iconography is readymade. In the case of *Snowman*, the act of creation is further deferred: the refrigerator is plugged in and a series of mechanical operations are carried out by the machine in order to produce the snowman inside of it. *Snowman* with Ben Vautier, *If Everything Is Sculpture, Why Make Sculpture? (Si tout est sculpture pourquoi faire de la sculpture?)*, 1995. Synthetic polymer paint on board

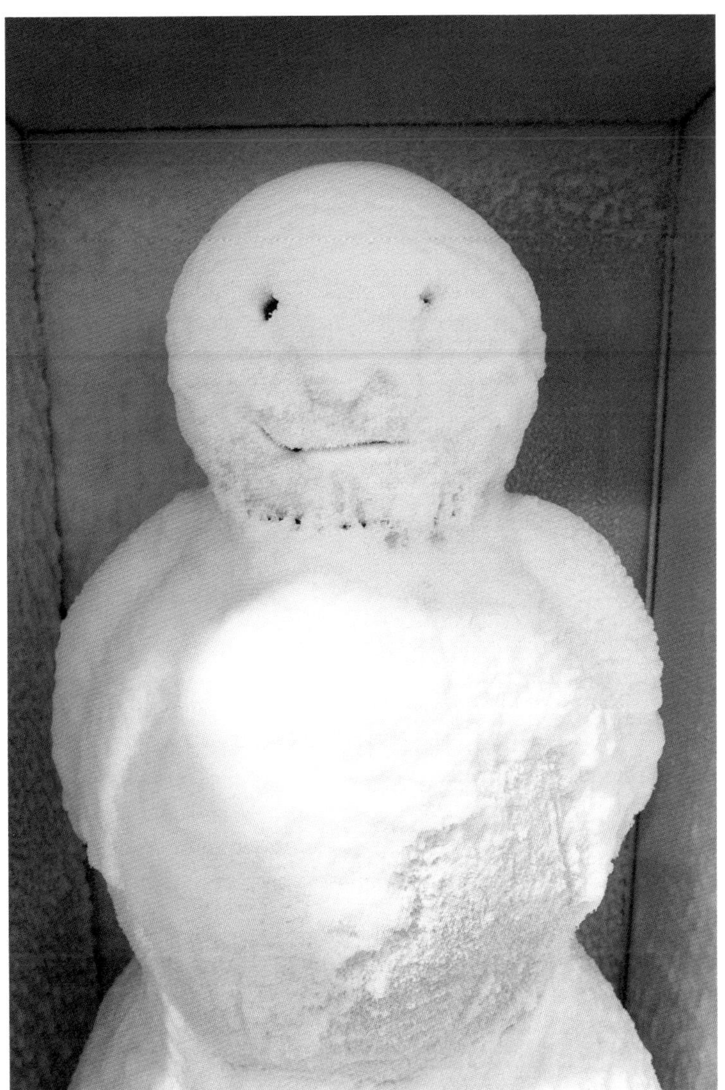

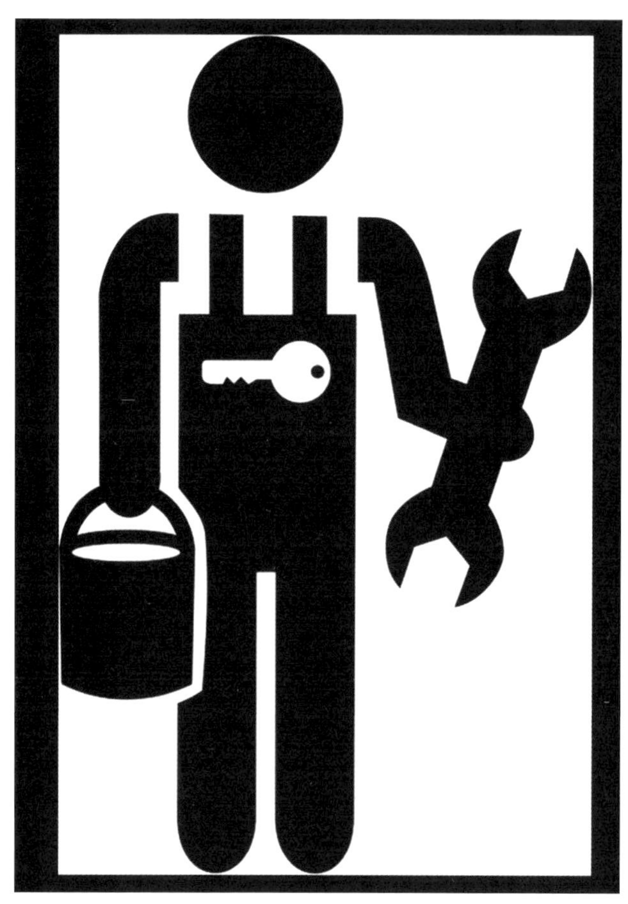

Reference images related to the topic of maintenance in museums, including climate-controlled vitrines and humidity and light-level measuring instruments

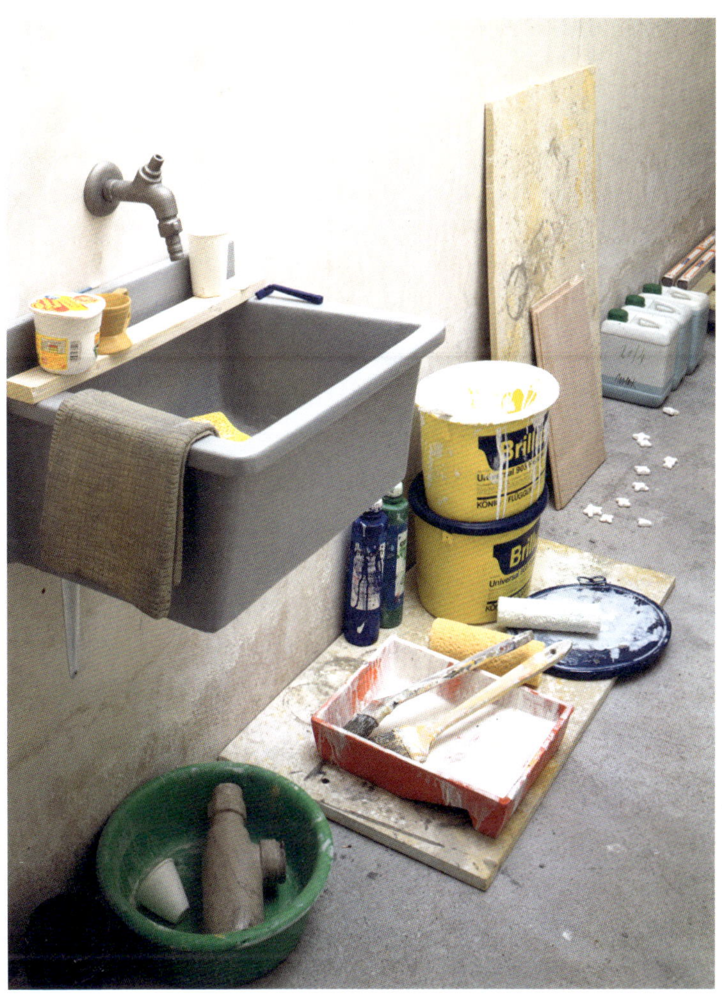

Hidden behind a door and visible through a small window, one finds a large number of sculptures of objects typically found in the janitor's closet of a museum. Cleaning products, wall paint, and packing materials are interspersed with personal items such as snacks and Aspirin. Fischli/Weiss, *Room under the Stairs*, 1993. Permanent installation at the Museum für moderne Kunst, Frankfurt. Carved and painted polyurethane

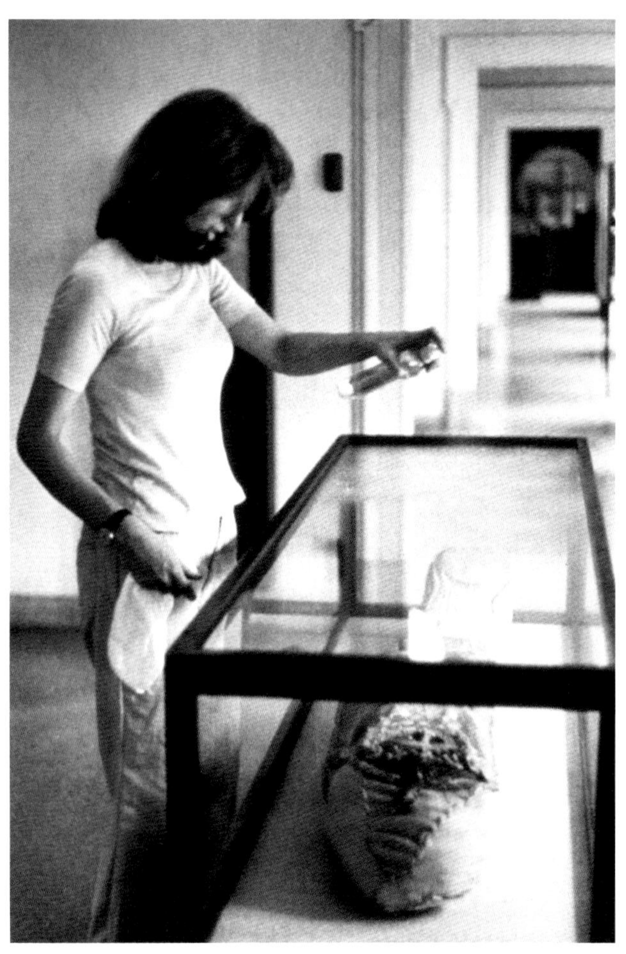

Mierle Laderman Ukeles, *Transfer: The Maintenance of the Art Object, Mummy Maintenance, with the Maintenance Man, the Maintenance Artist, and the Museum Conservator*, 1973. As formulated by the artist in her "Manifesto For Maintenance Art 1969!": "Two basic systems: Development and Maintenance … Development: pure individual creation; the new; change; progress; advance; excitement; flight or fleeing. Maintenance: keep the dust off the pure individual creation; preserve the new; sustain the change; protect progress; defend and prolong the advance; renew the excitement; repeat the flight."

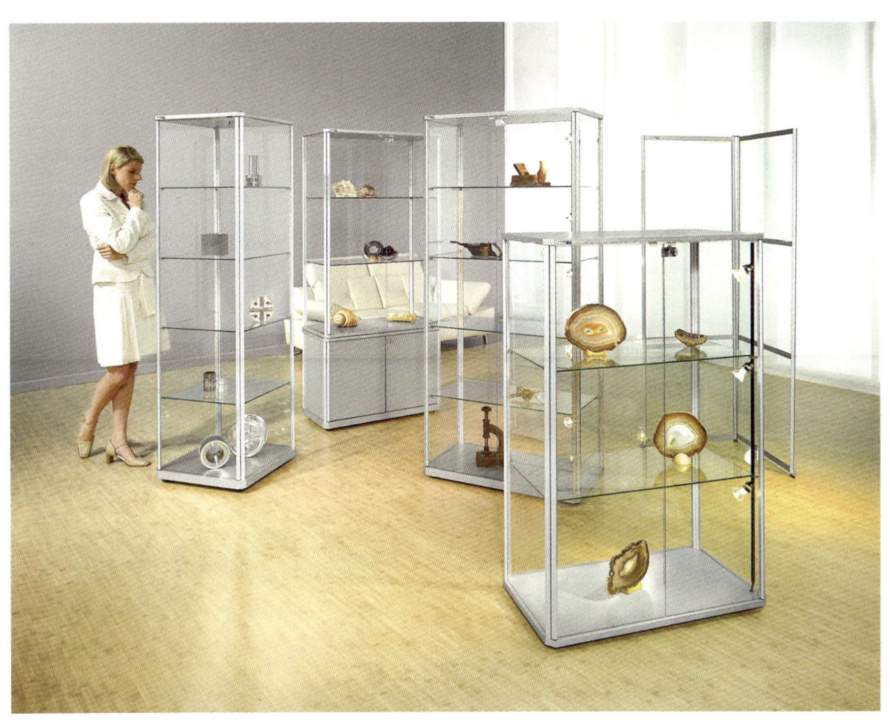

Promotional image for EUROKRAFTpro Design-Vitrine

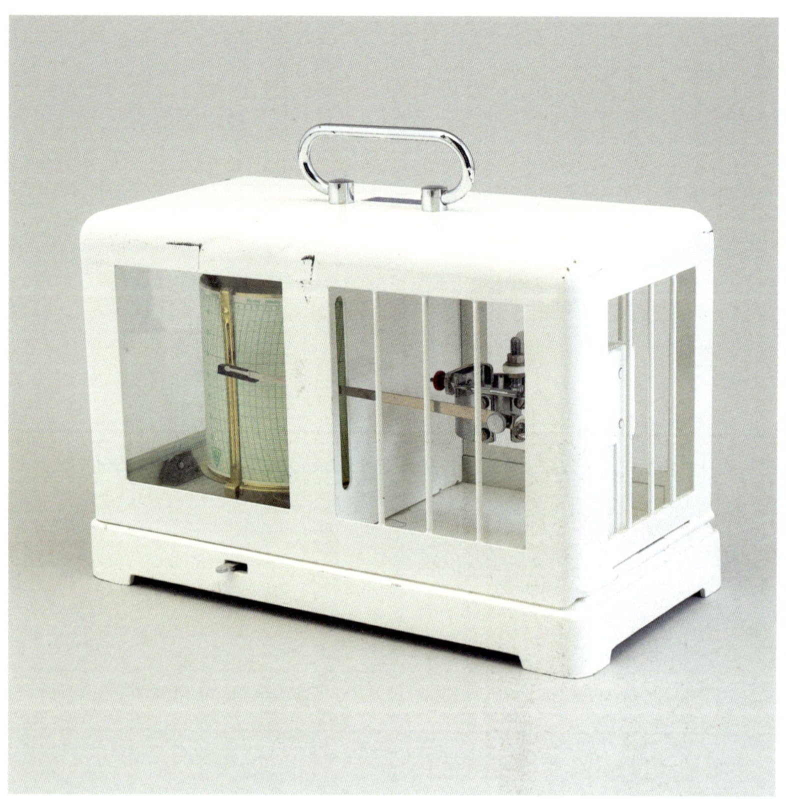

Snowman is a figure looked at inside of a vitrine, beheld like Frankenstein's monster in his laboratory tank or Snow White in her glass coffin. In addition to the constant electricity required to power the cooling unit that controls the fabrication and management of snow, *Snowman* needs care, maintenance, and appreciation from the outside world in order to survive. The participation of various staff members was therefore critical: art handlers to access the seemingly unopenable case with a hidden key; conservators to keep frost out of the snowman's eyes by wiping away built-up snow; and engineers to regulate the freezer's temperature to keep its body plump. Absent this labor of maintenance, the snowman would disappear, revealing its naked copper skeleton inside the vitrine, slowly becoming covered with dust and forgotten.

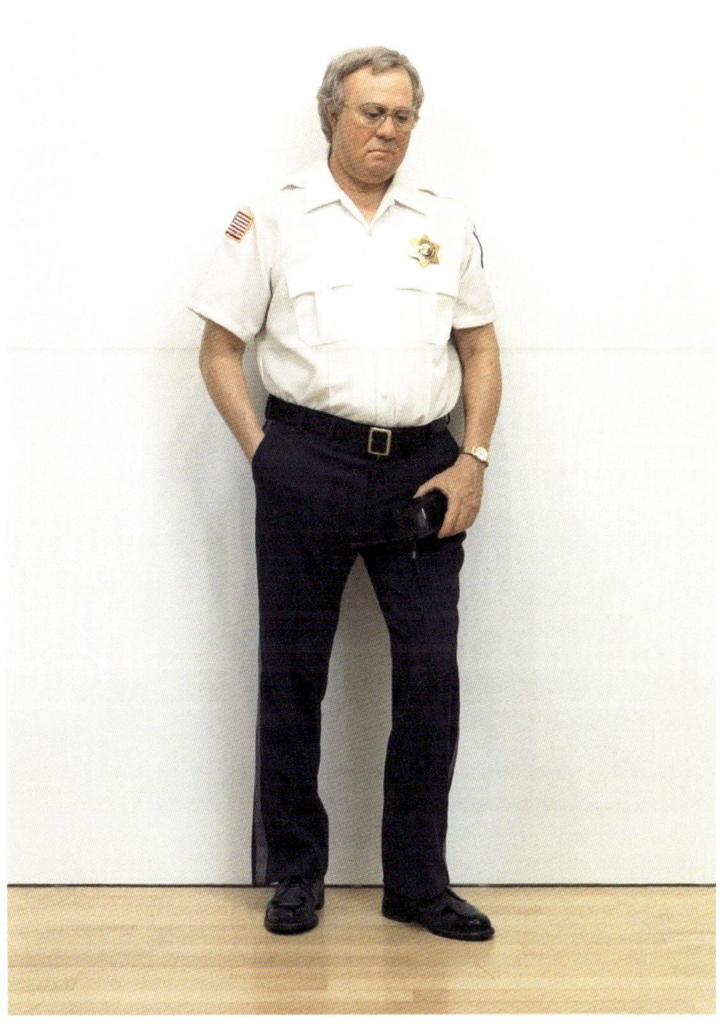

Duane Hanson, *Security Guard*, 1990. Autobody filler, polychromed in oil, with mixed media and accessories

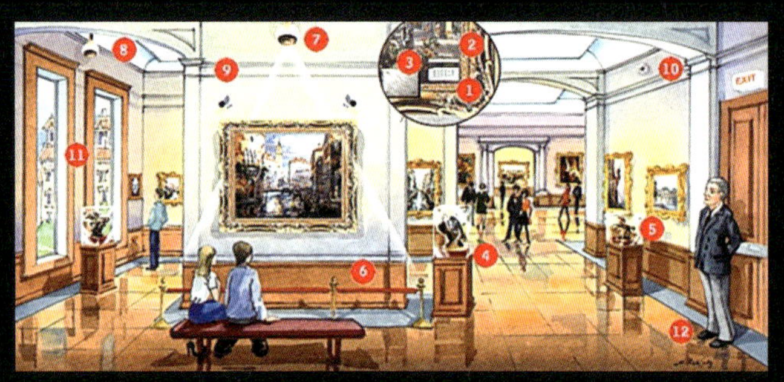

Art museum security: (1) Small and wireless, vibration sensors placed behind a painting can detect the lightest finger tap. (2) Inventory numbers written on the canvas back and recorded in a registrar's catalog. (3) At the bottom center of the painting, a metal boiler plate screws into both the frame and the wall. (4) Glazing protects some paintings. (5) Environmental sensors for fire, temperature changes and other hazards can be used to complement theft-deterrent sensors. (6) Around the edge of the room, a low rail creates a border discourages people from getting too close to the artwork (purely psychological). (7) Motion-detection devices beamed directly over the painting sound a chirping alarm to startle the too-close observer. (8) Saturation motion detection used in any given exhibit space. (9) Closed-circuit TV cameras. (10) Fire alarms, sprinklers and temperature controls are mandated in any exhibit space. (11) Windows fitted with alarms. (12) Security guards.

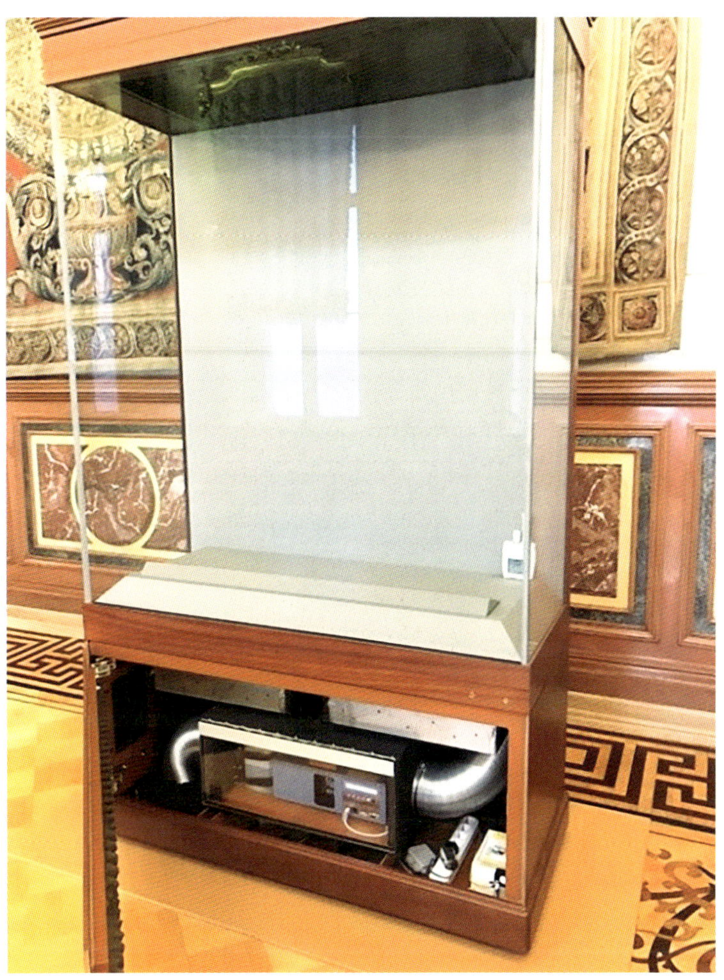

Instruments that measure and control temperature, humidity, and light levels of artworks on display in museums are often concealed in cleverly-constructed exhibition furniture or installed discreetly on nearby walls, and are monitored by staff after-hours. This institutional labor remains invisible to the public.

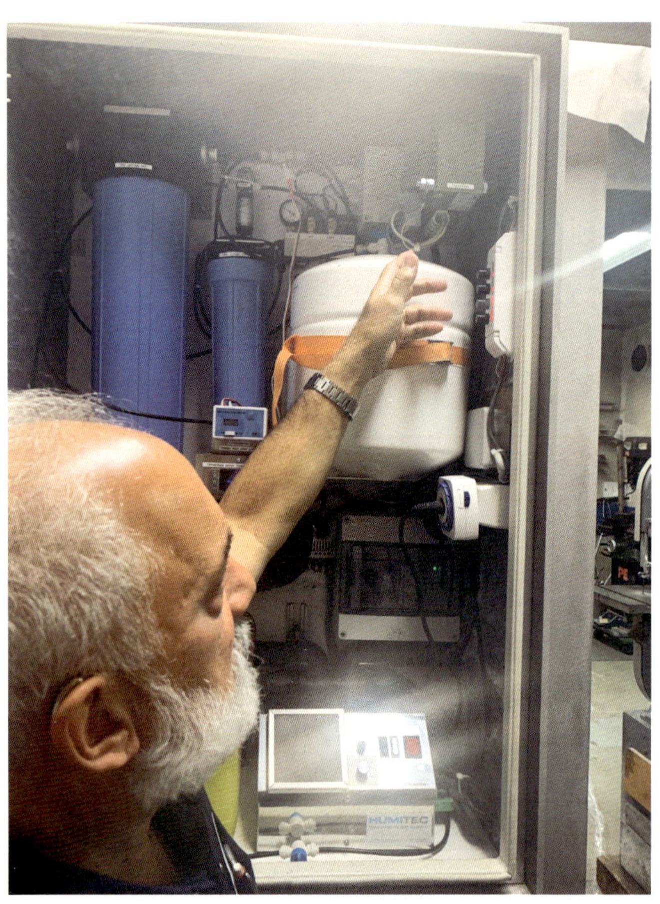

For the American presentation of *Snowman*, an electrical power conversion circuit with a transformer was installed in the control panel so that the 240-volt European refrigeration unit would operate on US line voltage (120 volts). Intermittent electrical failures suggested that the power demand of the refrigeration unit was overloading the conversion circuit. A permanent, reliable conversion for US line voltage was devised. The cooling unit was replaced with one designed for US power. Documentation of the replacement of the cooling system and LED lights for *Snowman* at Perfection Electricks, Bayonne, NJ

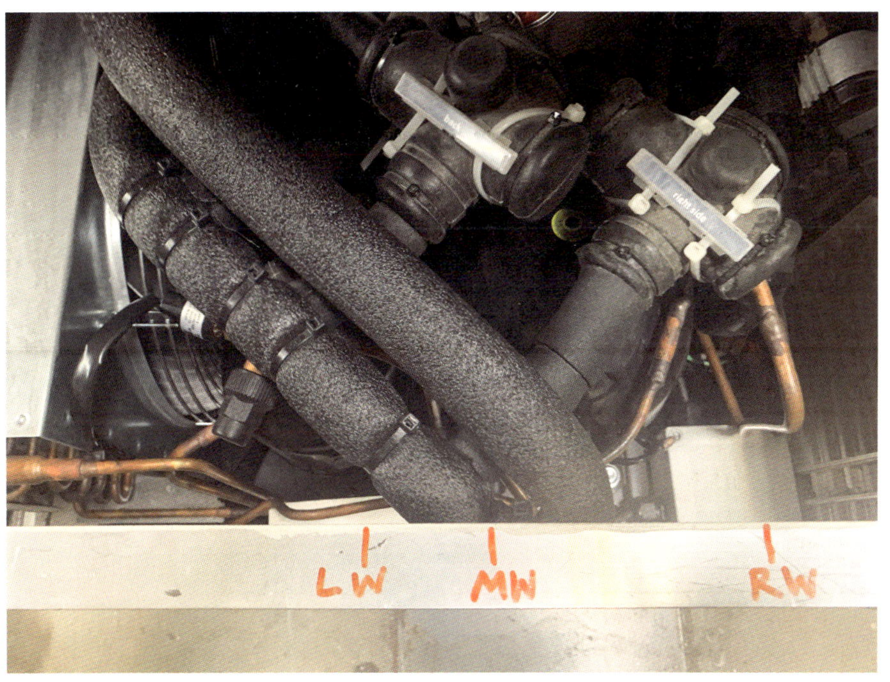
LW
MW
RW

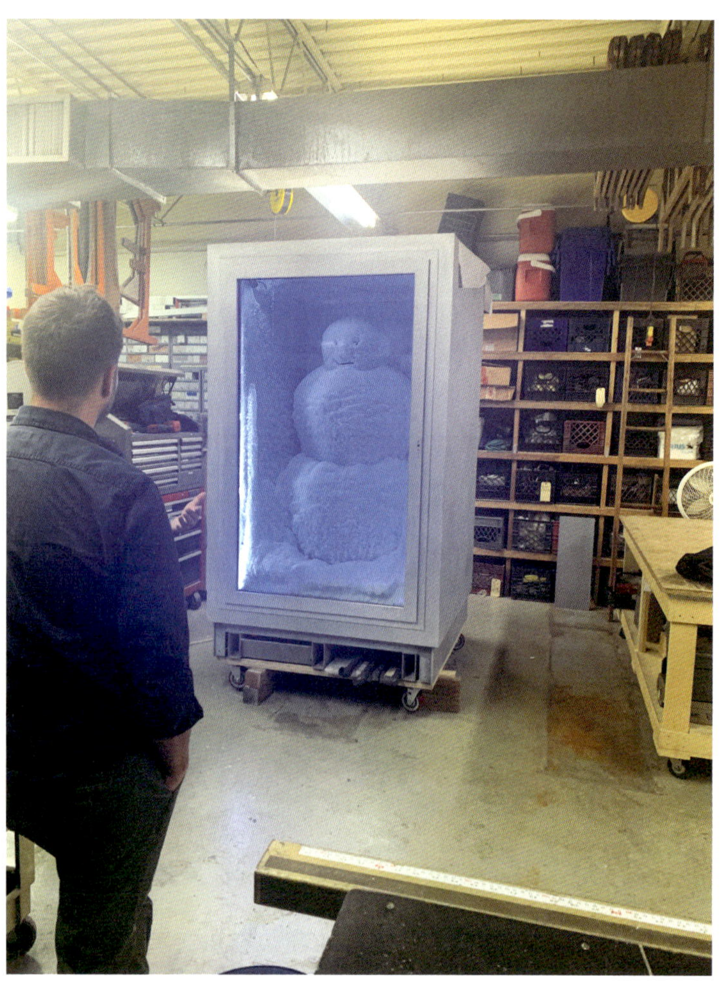

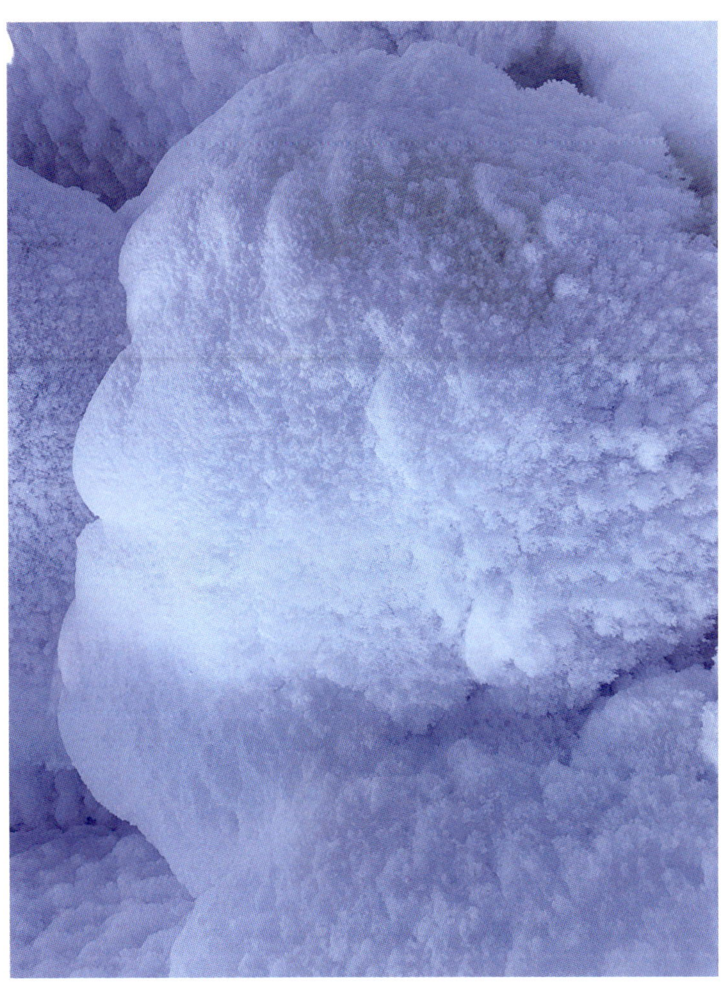

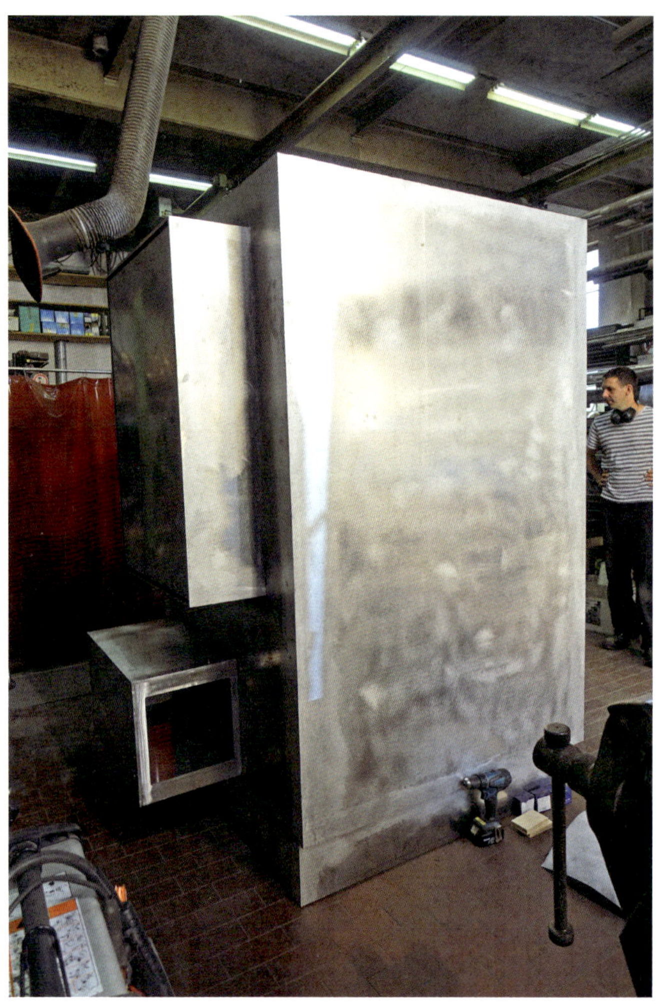

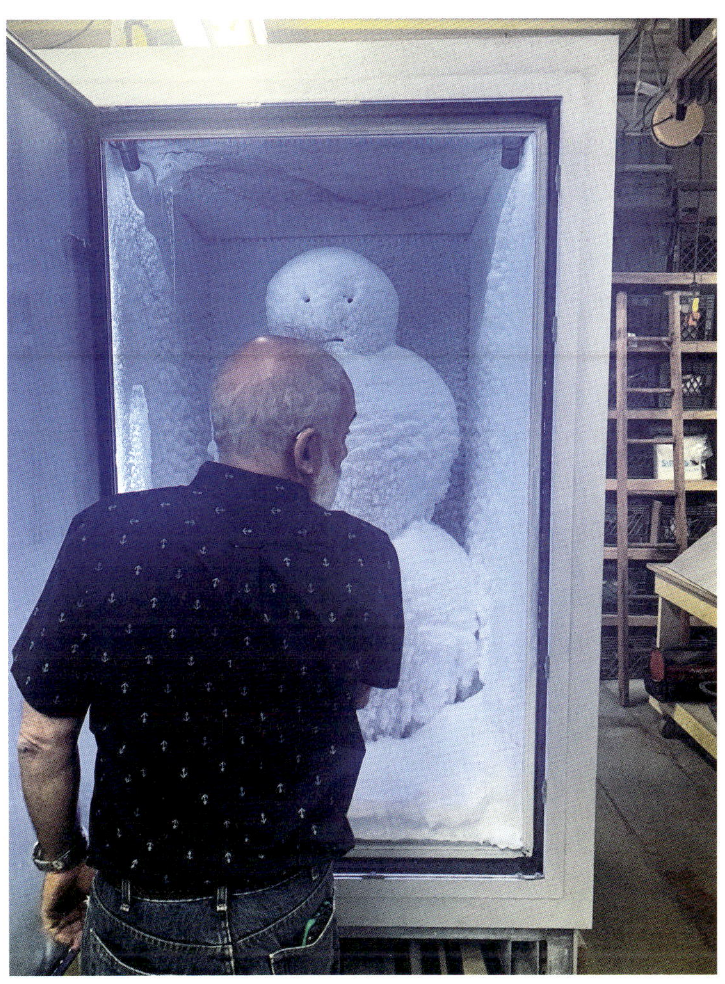

During transport, the two valves on the cooling unit were closed. Both valves must be opened before the further installation steps.
The cooling system can only be operated with open valves.
If uncertain, this should be carried out by a cooling technician.
(Transport preparations regarding refrigerant and valves are listed on page 54)

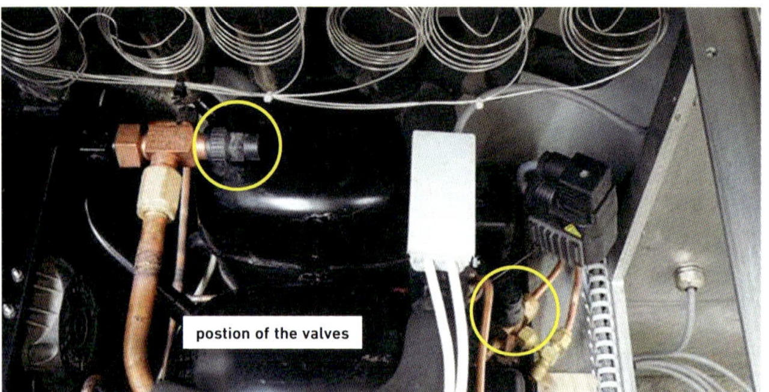

Closed valves

There are black protective caps on both valves. These protective caps must be unscrewed. The valves are closed when the copper square pins are turned clockwise all the way to the stop.

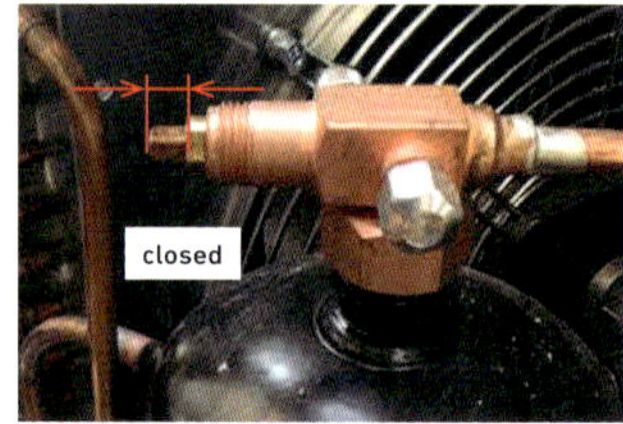

Opening the valves

To open the valves, remove the black protective caps. Then the copper square pins of both valves can be turned counterclockwise until they reach the stop. This allows the refrigerant to move throughout the entire cooling system again and further installation preparations can be carried out.

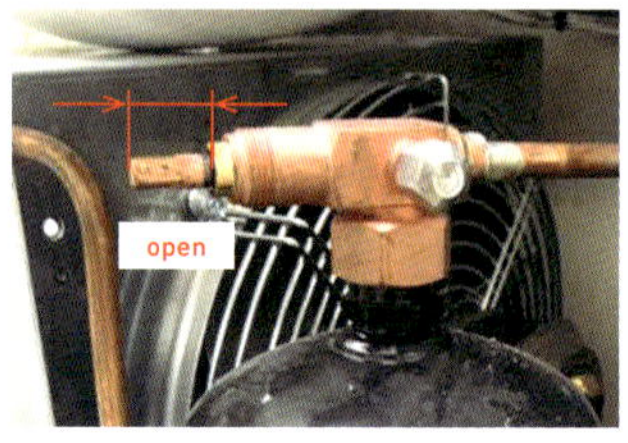

27 | 165 «Schneemann», 2019 by Fischli Weiss
2nd Production
Document created by Kunstgiesserei St.Gallen AG
Confidential Information

Excerpt from the technical installation, operation, and maintenance manual for *Snowman*, 2017/2022

Manual adjustment of frosting

The frosting at the snowman's eyes and mouth should be reduced manually if necessary. This means that if these areas freeze over to thickly, you can puncture the eyes with your finger and carefully retrace the line of the mouth.

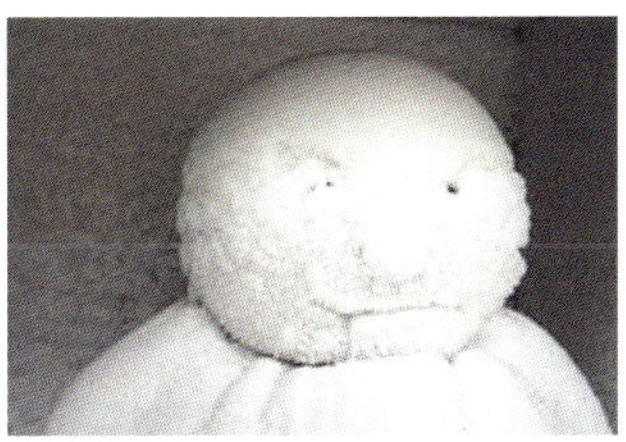

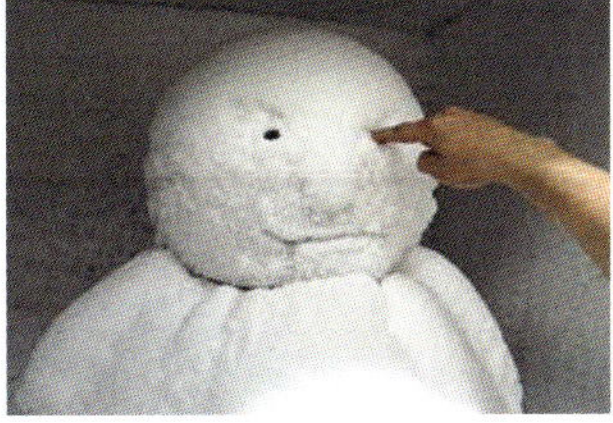

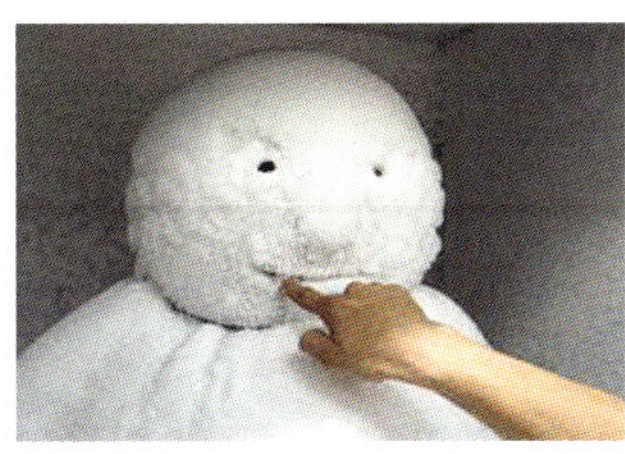

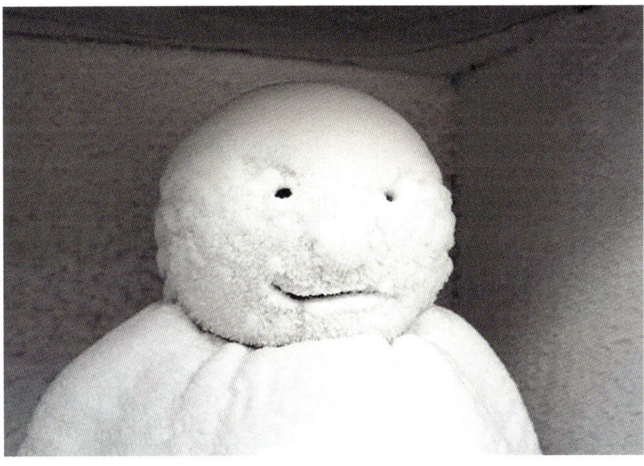

43 | 165 «Schneemann», 2019 by Fischli Weiss
2nd Production
Document created by Kunstgiesserei St.Gallen AG
Confidential Information

Excerpt from the technical manual instructing conservators how corrections can be made in the facial expressions, as necessary

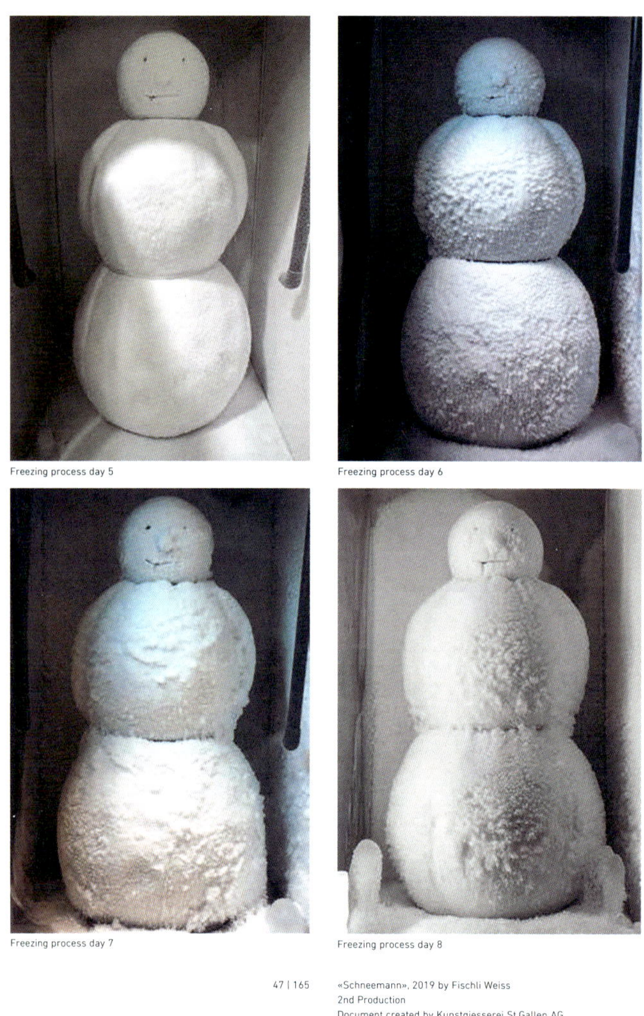
Freezing process day 5

Freezing process day 6

Freezing process day 7

Freezing process day 8

47 | 165

«Schneemann», 2019 by Fischli Weiss
2nd Production
Document created by Kunstgiesserei St.Gallen AG
Confidential Information

Excerpt from the technical manual demonstrating how ice and snow builds up over several days after the cooling units are powered on

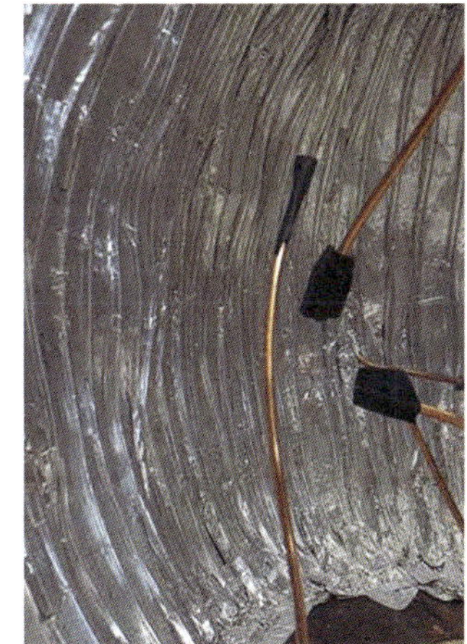
Installing the cooling pipes

Cooling Technology

Important: servicing of the cooling unit may only be executed by a specialist cooling technician.

Expansion valves

The expansion valves for the snowman are located inside the snowman figure. The six expansion valves for the three refrigerator walls are located in the lower control cabinet. The roof and floor of the refrigerator do not contain any cooling systems.

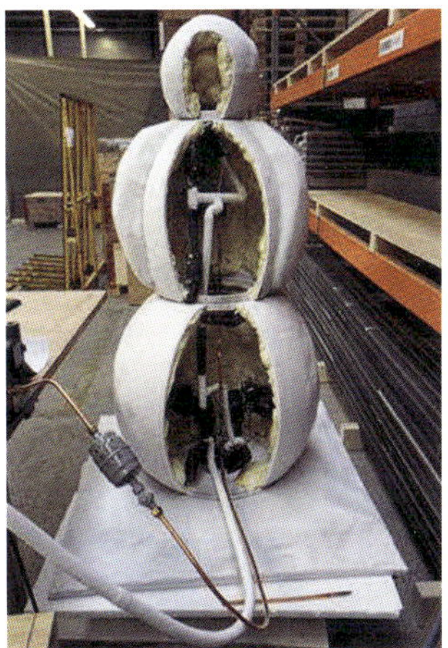

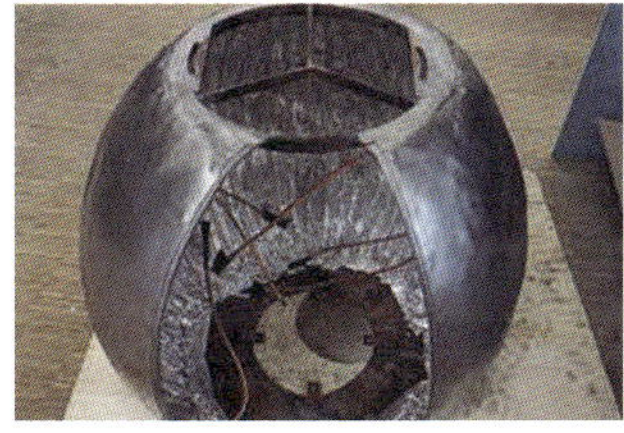

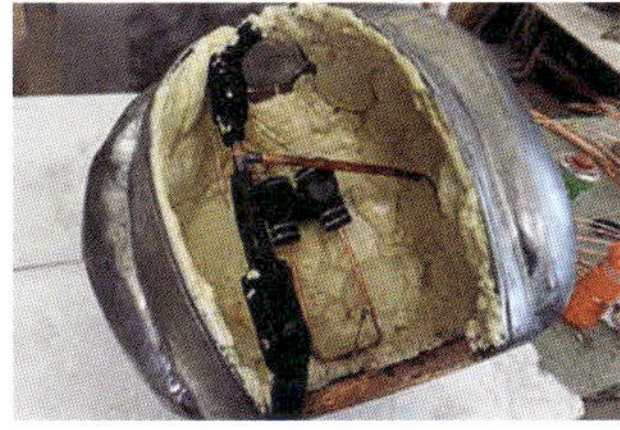

55 | 165 «Schneemann», 2019 by Fischli Weiss
2nd Production
Document created by Kunstgiesserei St.Gallen AG
Confidential Information

Excerpt from the technical manual showing details of the cooling mechanism inside the snowman's copper skeleton

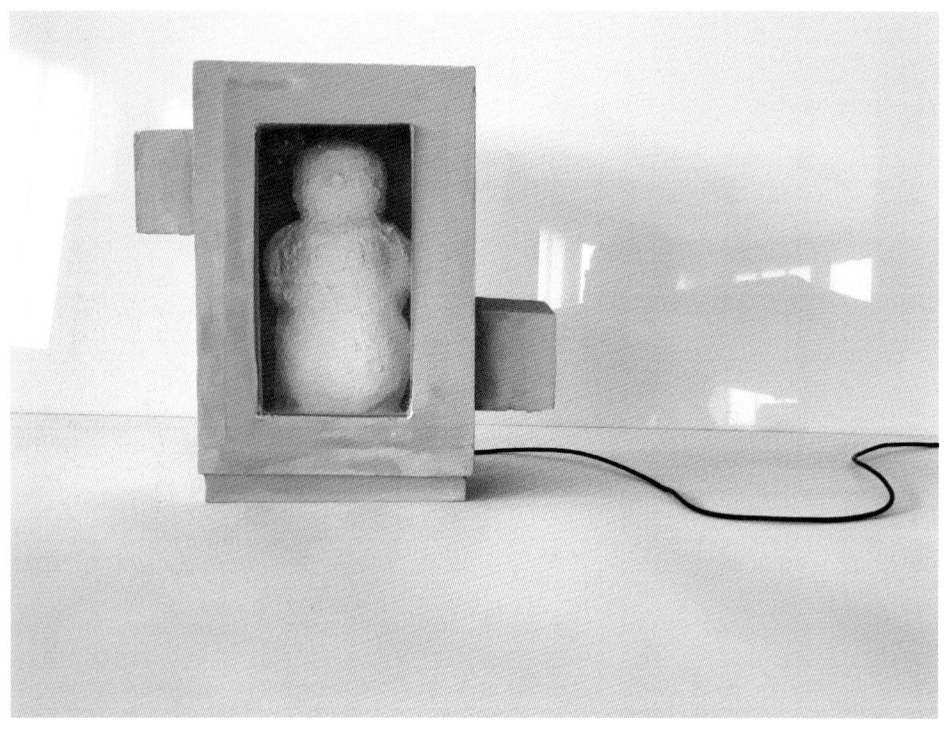

A single variant version of *Snowman* was devised in 2019. For this iteration, the cooling system apparatus was made visible on both sides of the refrigerator and the glass vitrine window was made smaller. The overall configuration is more machinelike, yet also more figurative, with the organic, representational, vertically tripartite form of the snowman positioned within the abstract, geometric, horizontally tripartite form of the refrigerator. Polyurethane model in 1:20 scale for variation of Snowman, 2019

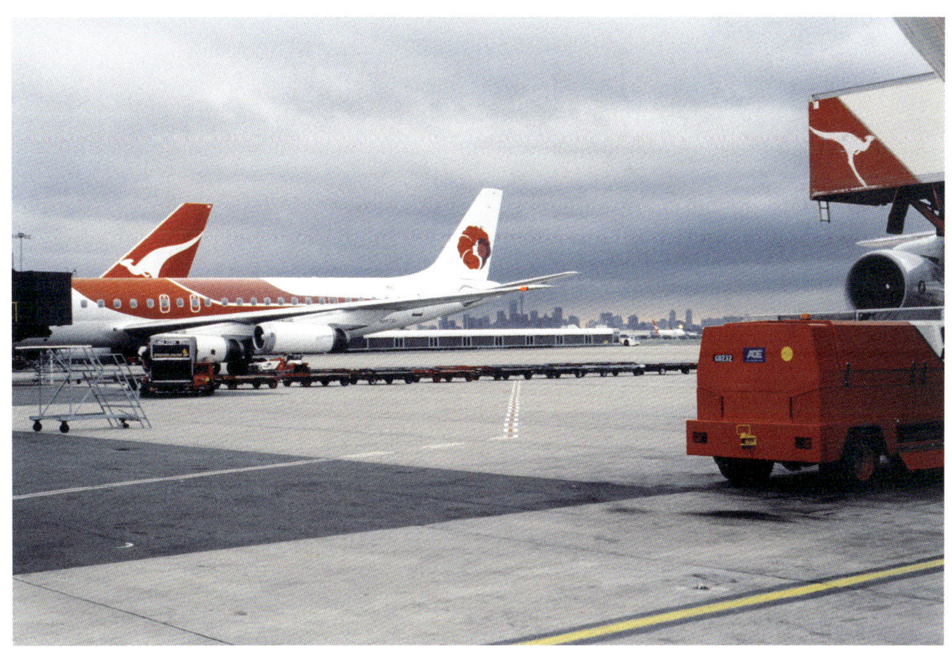

Between 1987 and 2012 Fischli/Weiss made a series of more than 1,000 photographs of the banal aspects of airports, such as planes waiting on the tarmac, fuel vehicles, and baggage trucks. The project was documented in the 2012 book *800 Views of Airports*. Fischli/Weiss, *Airport (Sydney – Quantas)*, 1987–2012. Photographic C-print

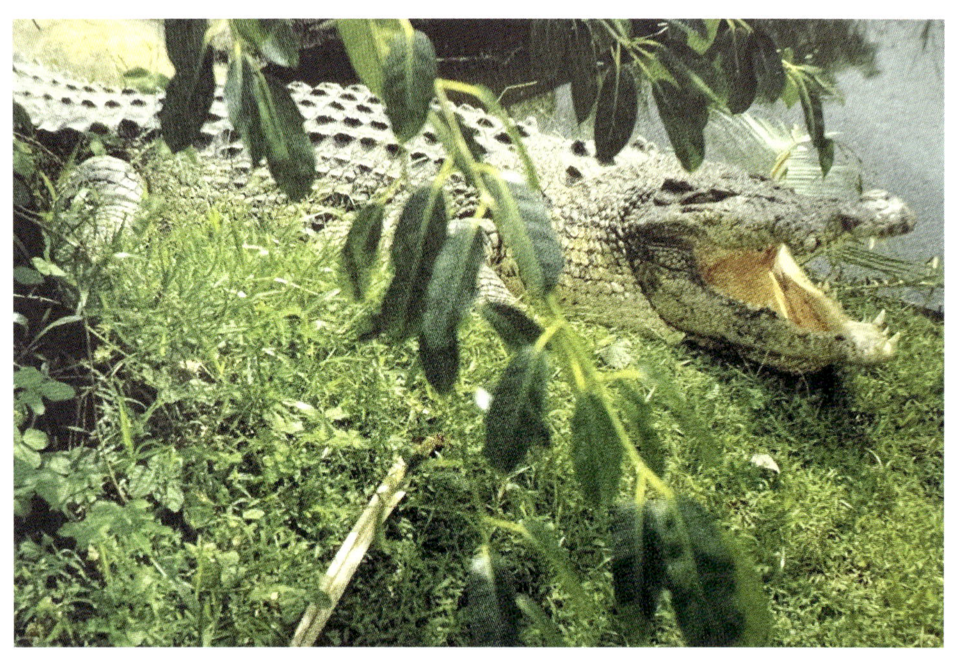

Between 1986 and 2012, Fischli / Weiss made a series of more than 3,000 photographs at international tourist destinations on all seven continents, titled *Visible World*. The project has been presented as standalone photographs, illuminated color slides laid out on tables, video slideshow projections, and an artist's book. Fischli / Weiss, photograph from *Visible World*, 1986–2012

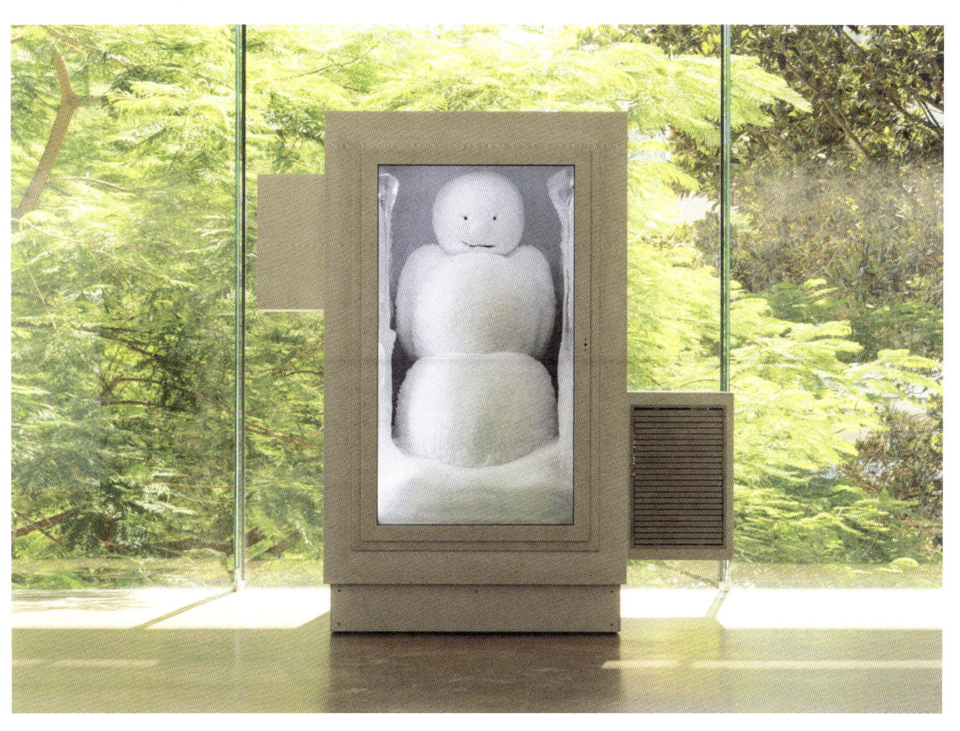

Snowman installed at the Queensland Gallery of Modern Art, Brisbane, Australia, 2019

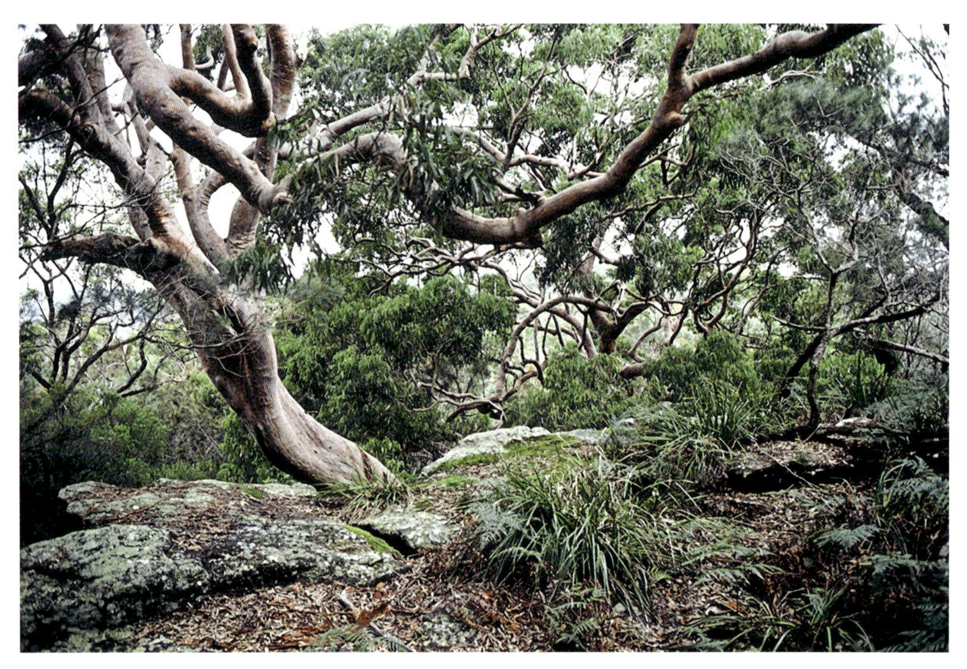

Fischli / Weiss, photograph from *Visible World*, 1986–2012

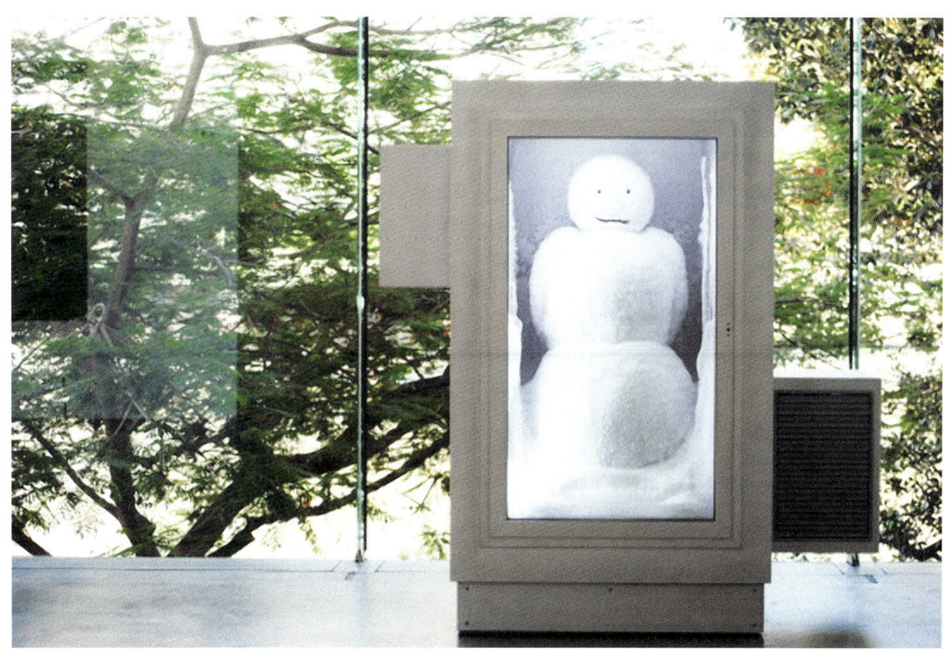

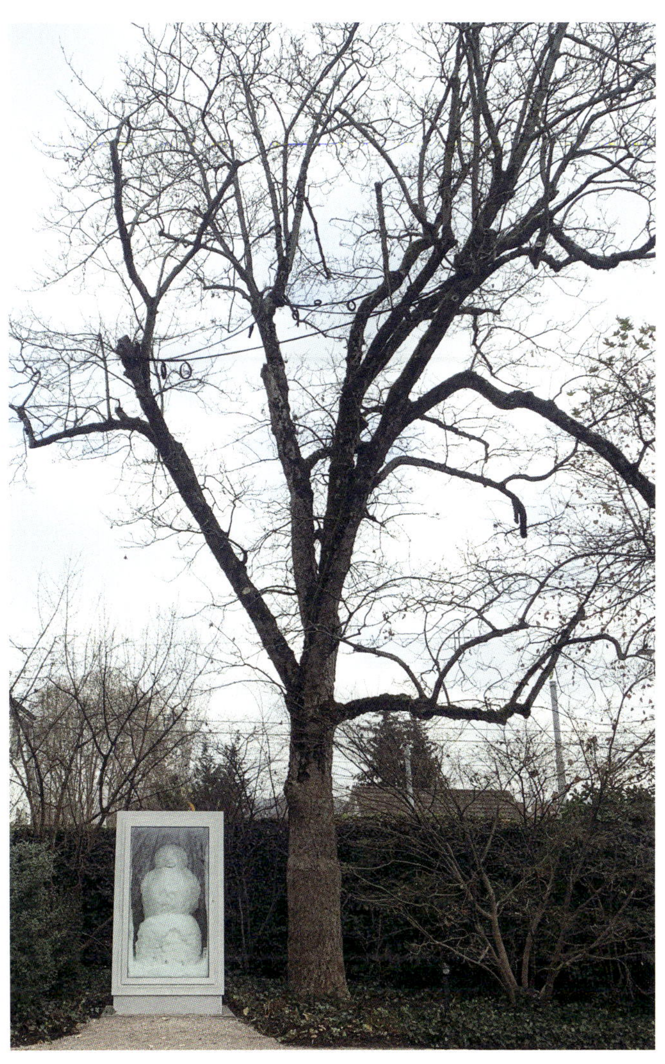

Snowman installed in the park at Fondation Beyeler, Basel, Switzerland, November 2020–ongoing. Organized by Theodora Vischer

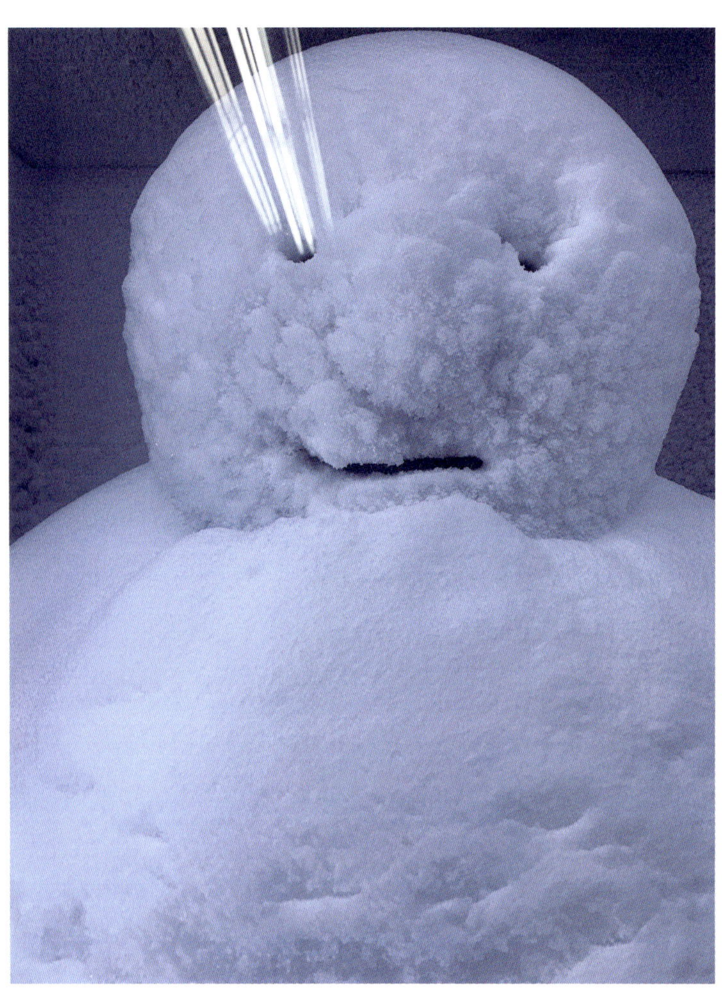

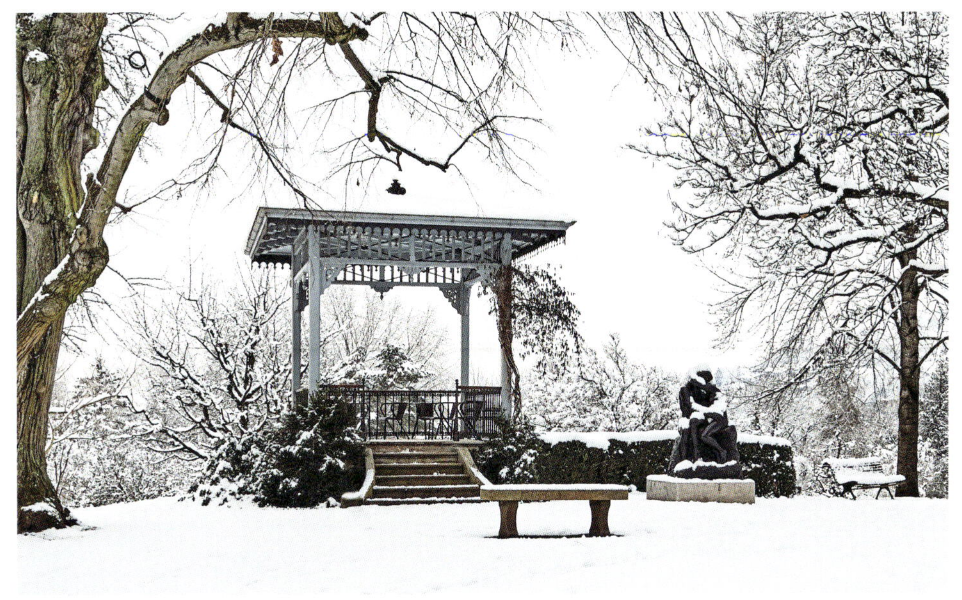

At Fondation Beyeler, *Snowman* is placed in a classical park, a setting where nature is shaped and maintained by human hands and protected by walls. The landscape is planned and manicured. Gardeners prune unruly trees, clean the ponds from time to time, and plant tastefully selected flowers each season. Typical of parks since André Le Nôtre's aesthetic formulations of landscape design in the mid-seventeenth century, this one is equipped with paths, benches, sculptures, and a pavilion meant to facilitate leisurely strolls and moments of rest. Increasingly in the twentieth century, the park has come to be referred to as the "green lung" of a city, for the healthy environment it provides for urban inhabitants as a place where one can go during lunch break to eat a snack, take a walk, or smoke a cigarette.

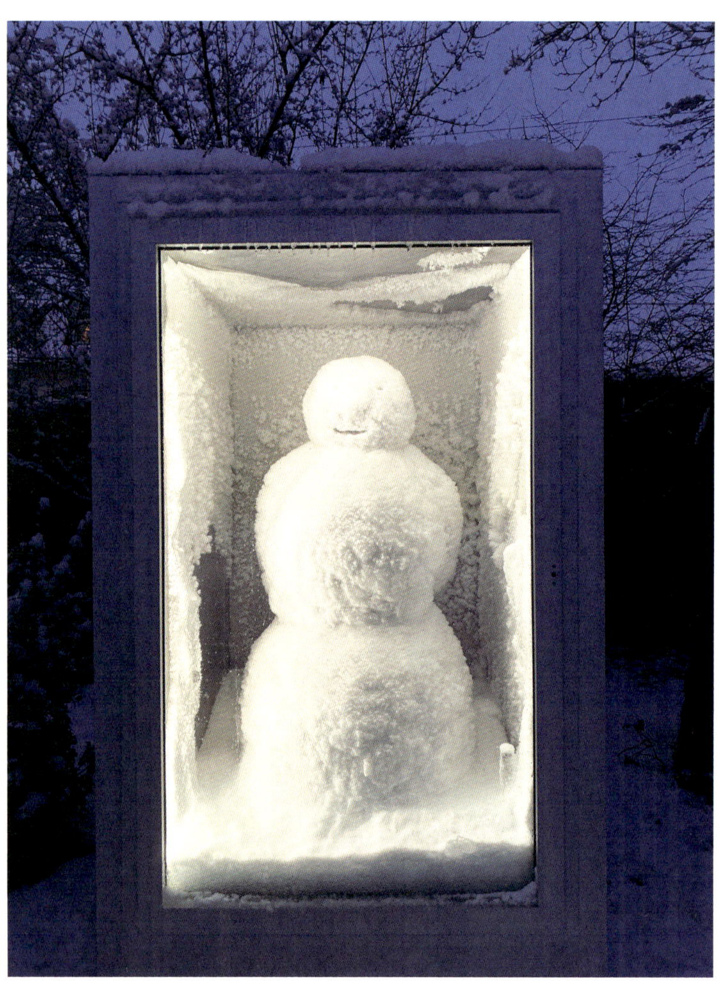

As is the case at the Heizkraftwerk Römerbrücke in Saarbrücken, in Basel *Snowman* is placed at the entrance of the Beyeler park, where it serves as its passive gatekeeper.

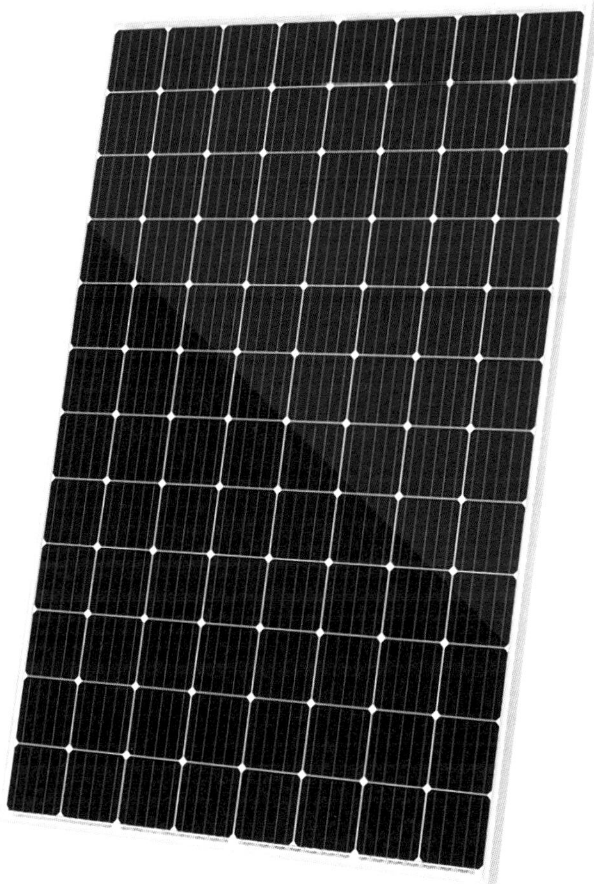

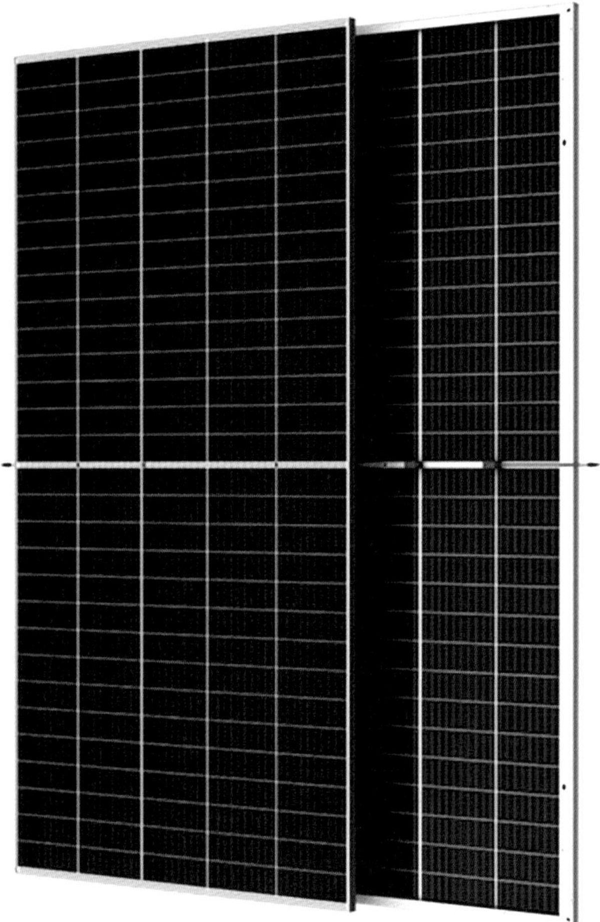

Snowman was technically reconfigured to run on solar power for its presentation at Fondation Beyeler. As it happens, the solar panels generate the maximum energy output on a sunny, hot summer day—exactly the kind of day on which *Snowman* most desperately needs to be kept cold.

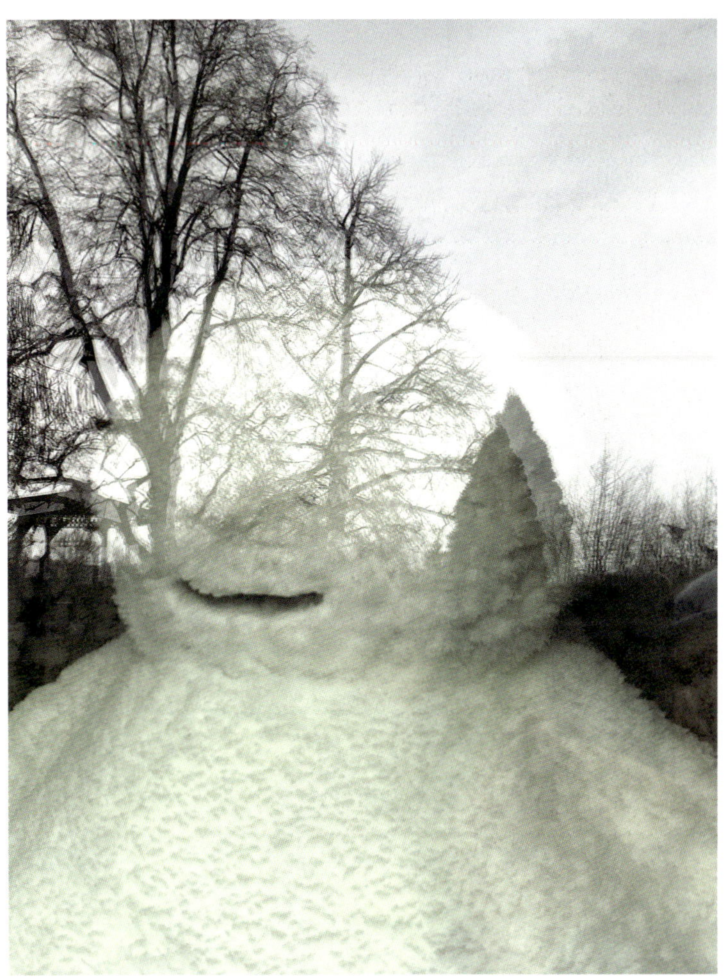

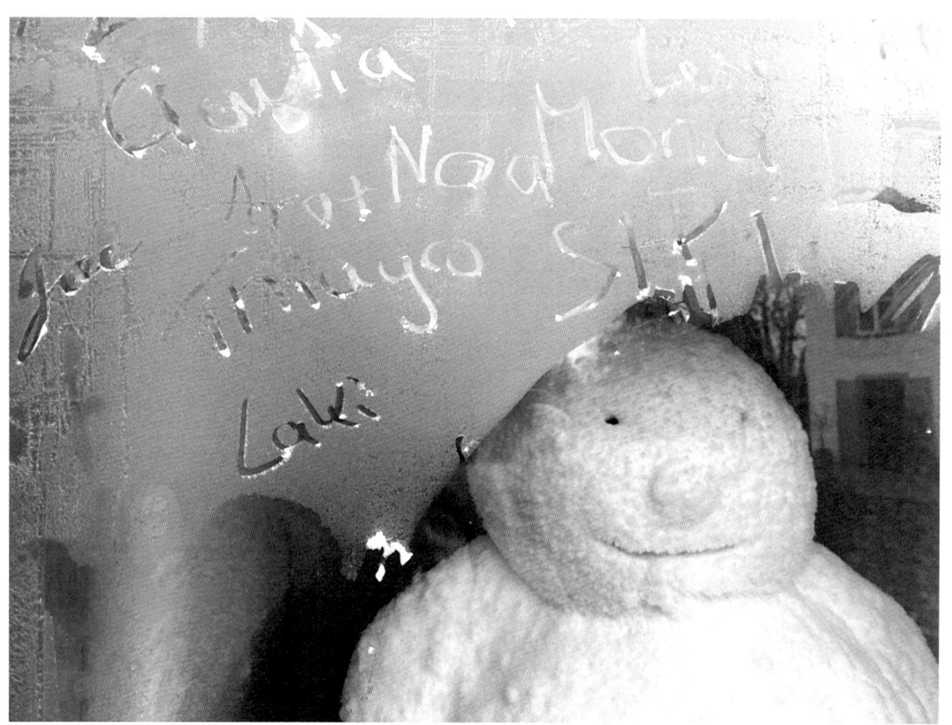

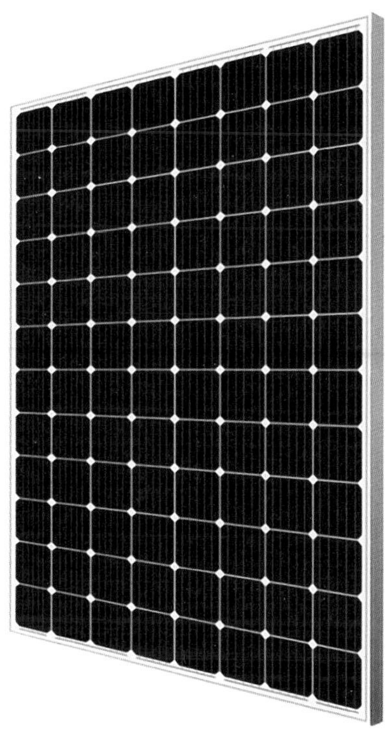

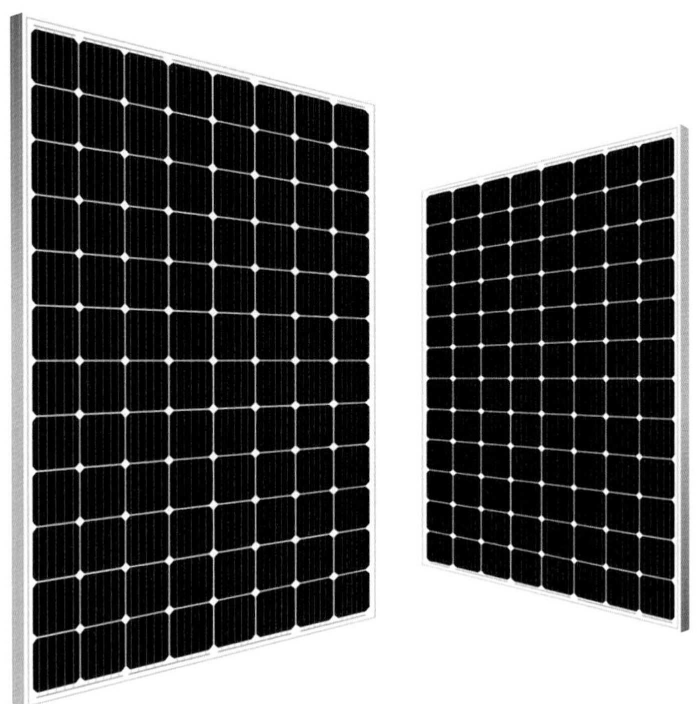

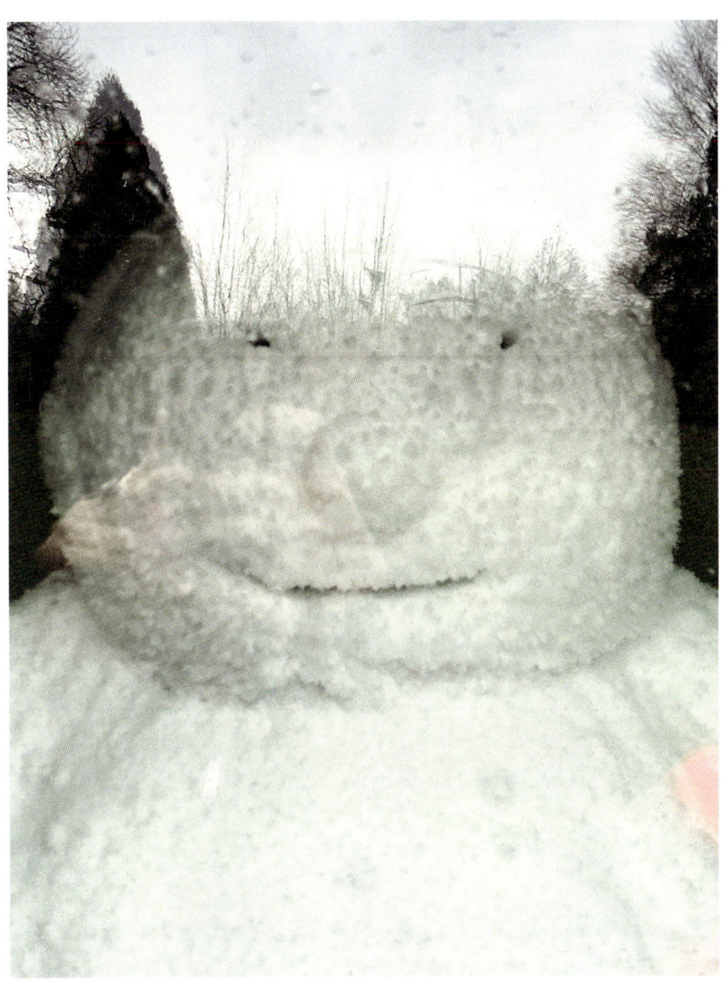

For its survival, the snowman must remain trapped in its cozy freezer, unable to explore the surrounding environment. Interactions with the outside world, then, only occur in the double exposures that can be seen in reflections of the vitrine glass.

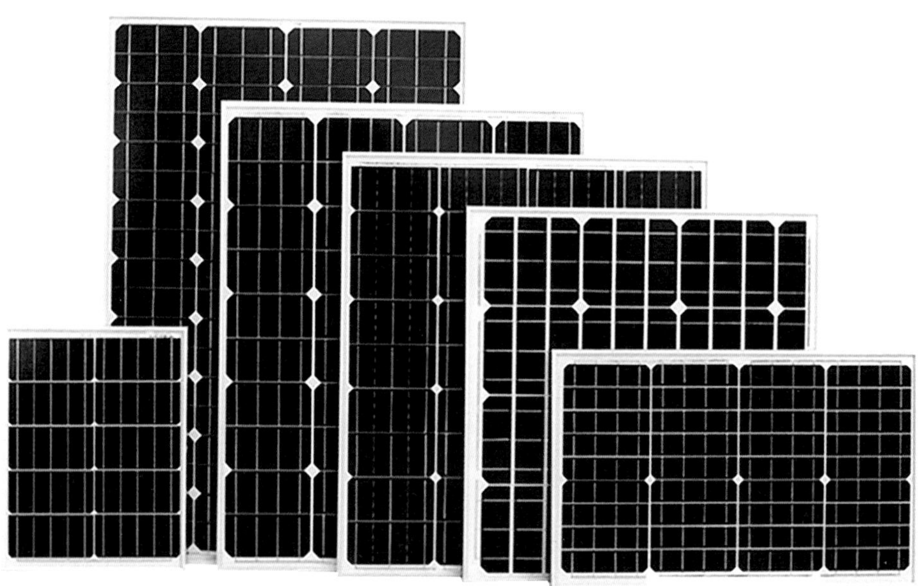

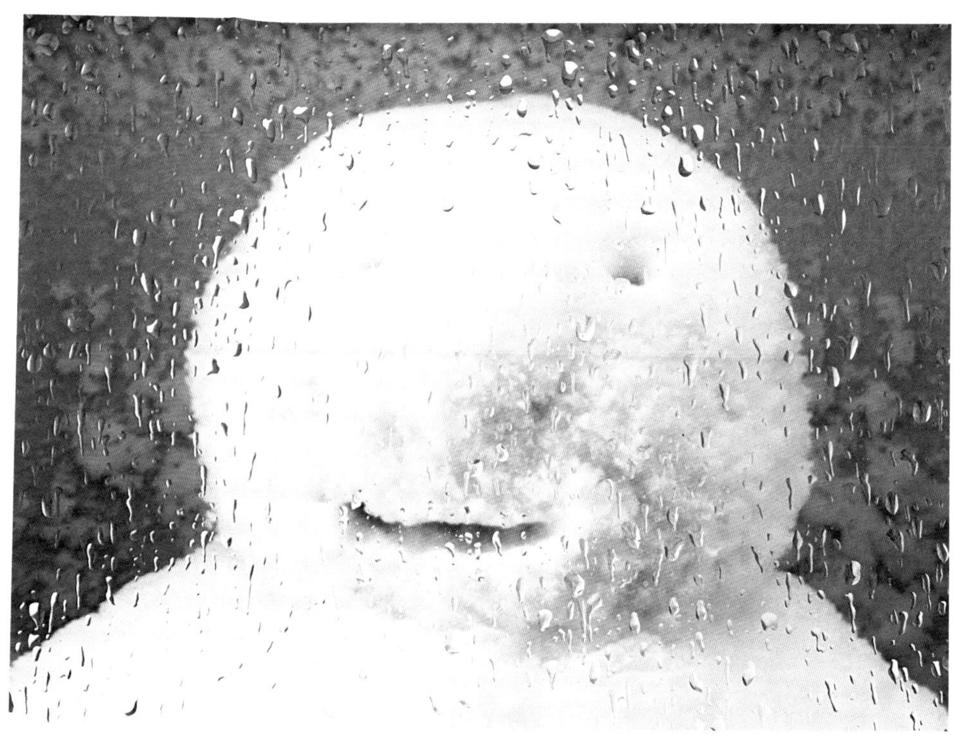

Snowman (1987/2016) is an edition of two with one artist's proof. These works are in the collections of The Museum of Modern Art, New York (Gift of The Riklis Collection of McCrory Corporation (by exchange), and Committee on Painting and Sculpture Funds, 2018); S. Mueller Family, Cleveland; and Fondation Beyeler, Riehen/Basel. A single variation is in the collection of the Queensland Gallery of Modern Art, Brisbane (Purchased 2019 with funds from Tim Fairfax AC through the Queensland Art Gallery, Gallery of Modern Art Foundation).

Peter Fischli is an artist and, from 2014 to 2018, taught at the Städelschule, Frankfurt. From 1979 to 2012, he collaborated with David Weiss. The art of Fischli/Weiss has been the subject of large-scale retrospectives at museums across North America and Europe, such as the Solomon R. Guggenheim Museum, New York (2016), and Tate Modern, London (2006–07), among many others. Fischli's recent solo projects include exhibitions at the Fondazione Prada (2021), Kunsthaus Bregenz (2020), The Museum of Modern Art (2018), the Aspen Art Museum (2017), and Fondation Beyeler (2016). He lives in Zurich.

Cara Manes is Associate Curator in the Department of Painting and Sculpture at The Museum of Modern Art. There, she has organized numerous exhibitions, including a recent survey of the work of Alexander Calder, and *Artist's Choice* shows with Trisha Donnelly and Peter Fischli. She lives in Brooklyn.

Photo Credits
akg-images: p. 89; Archiv Energie SaarLorLux AG, Saarbrücken, photo: Anke Jacob: p. 43; © Bil Bowen – USA TODAY: p. 48; bpk/Hamburger Kunsthalle/Elke Walford: p. 23; © David A. Brichford, courtesy of The Cleveland Museum of Art: pp. 118–119; Courtesy of Jana Euler and dépendance, Brussels: p. 39; Fischli/Weiss Archive: pp. 4–6, 8, 13, 15–22, 24–28, 30–31, 47, 49, 57–60, 64–65, 69–77, 80, 83, 85, 90–98, 101–102, 104–107, 110–113, 115–117, 120–135, 137, 144–156, 158, 161–162, 164; Courtesy the Estate of Duane Hanson and Gagosian, photo: Robert McKeever: p. 141; Merrill Kelley: p. 86; © Mierle Laderman Ukeles: p. 138; Mark Niedermann: p. 163; © Pictorial Press LTD/Alamy Stock Photo: p. 88; © Queensland Art Gallery/Gallery of Modern Art, photo: Chloë Callistemon: p. 157; Rijksmuseum, Amsterdam: p. 79
Front cover image by Gina Fischli

Editor
Peter Fischli

Concept and Texts
Peter Fischli and Cara Manes

Copyediting
Aaron Bogart

Graphic design and Typesetting
Teo Schifferli

Production
Lösch GmbH & Co. KG

Published by
Verlag der Buchhandlung Walther und Franz König
Ehrenstraße 4, D-50672 Köln

The authors thank the following people: Amelie Baader, Gabriel Badertscher, Marty Chafkin, Stephanie Dorsey, Gina Fischli, Lukas Furrer, Gary Garrels, Susanne Ghez, Ann Goldstein, Ryan Hart, Bernhard Hegglin, Jochem Jourdan, Sam Keller, Jason Klimatsas, Kasper König, Walther König, Damasia Lacroze, Felix Lehner, Ben Ludwig, Philomene Magers, Matthew Marks, Charlotte Matter, Bernhard Müller, Michel Parasol, Eva Presenhuber, Pascal Schneuwly, Monika Sprüth, Ann Temkin, and Theodora Vischer.

Peter Fischli thanks all the photographers whose works have become part of this collage and who could not be identified or located.

Bibliographic information published by the Deutsche Nationalbibliothek
The Deutsche Nationalbibliothek lists this publication in the Deutsche Nationalbibliografie; detailed bibliographic data are available in the Internet at http://dnb.d-nb.de.

Printed in Germany

Distribution

Germany, Austria, Switzerland
Buchhandlung Walther König
Ehrenstraße 4,
D-50672 Köln
Tel: +49 (0) 221/20 59 6 53
verlag@buchhandlung-walther-koenig.de

Unites States and Canada
D.A.P. / Distributed Art Publishers, Inc.
75 Broad Street, Suite 630
USA - New York, NY 10004
Fon +1 (0) 212 627 1999
orders@dapinc.com

Outside the United States and Canada,
Germany, Austria and Switzerland by
Thames & Hudson Ltd., London
www.thamesandhudson.com

ISBN 978-3-7533-0250-8